Que® Quick Reference Series

UNIX® Shell Commands Quick Reference

William Holliker

Que® Corporation
Carmel, Indiana

Library of Congress Catalog Number: 90-61526

ISBN 0-88022-572-6

93 92 91   5 4 3

Interpretation of the printing code: the rightmost double-digit number is the year of the book's printing; the rightmost single-digit number is the number of the book's printing. For example, a printing code of 89-4 shows that the fourth printing of the book occurred in 1989.

Information in this book is based on UNIX System V, Release 3.

Que Quick Reference Series

The *Que Quick Reference Series* is a portable resource of essential microcomputer knowledge. Whether you are a new or experienced user, you can rely on the high-quality information contained in these convenient guides.

Drawing on the experience of many of Que's best-selling authors, the *Que Quick Reference Series* helps you easily access important program information. Now it's easy to look up programming information for assembly language, C, DOS and BIOS functions, QuickBASIC 4, Turbo Pascal, and UNIX as well as frequently used commands and functions for 1-2-3, WordPerfect 5, MS-DOS, dBASE IV, and AutoCAD.

Use the *Que Quick Reference Series* as a compact alternative to confusing and complicated traditional documentation.

The *Que Quick Reference Series* also includes these titles:

Programming Books Director
Allen L. Wyatt, Sr.

Product Development Specialist
Linda Sanning

Technical Editors
Jim Carr
Don Gloistein

Production
Ann K. Taylor

Trademark Acknowledgments
Que Corporation has made every effort to supply trademark information about company names, products, and services mentioned in this book. Trademarks indicated below were derived from various sources. Que Corporation cannot attest to the accuracy of this information.

UNIX is a registered trademark of AT&T.

Table of Contents

INTRODUCTION

The UNIX *shell* is both a command interpreter and programming language. Two versions of the shell run under UNIX System V: the *Bourne shell* developed by Steven Bourne, and the newer *Korn shell* developed by David F. Korn, both of AT&T Bell Laboratories. The Korn shell, commonly referred to as *ksh*, has all the features of the Bourne shell (*sh*), some of the best features of the *C shell* (the UCB 4.X version of the shell, developed by Bill Joy at the University of California at Berkeley), and many new features of its own.

This book is intended to serve as a quick reference guide to the features of the Bourne and Korn shells. The Korn shell supports all Bourne shell features. In most cases, there are no differences between the Bourne shell syntax and Korn shell syntax for a command. Any differences, as well as commands that apply only to the Korn shell, are indicated specifically with the notation **KSH only.**

Shell programming relies to a great extent on the numerous commands provided on a UNIX system. Knowing these commands and their use is invaluable when you develop shell programs. Some of the more common UNIX commands are discussed in this guide; however, you should have the *AT&T UNIX User's Reference Manual* available while you develop shell programs.

This book contains many examples of shell commands that can be used both directly from the command line or as part of shell scripts. Shell programming is limited only by your creativity.

How To Use This Book

This book is organized into the following sections:

"Shell Basics" explains the fundamentals of the Bourne and Korn shells. Topics include how to enter simple, sequential, and group commands; the use of the shell metacharacters; input and output redirection; pipelines; and the shell environment. You can use this section to quickly locate the syntax of any shell convention.

"Shell Files and Processes" explains how the UNIX file system and process control mechanism can help you make the best use of the shell.

"Built-In Commands" explains commands built into the Bourne and Korn shells.

"Shell Parameters and Variables" contains information for using shell parameters and variables, including any predefined variables and their default values. Also included are notations for constructing and using conditional parameter substitution.

"Programming Constructs" provides information about using the shell's built-in programming constructs `for`, `while`, `until`, `if`, `case`, `functions`, `select`, and `time`.

"Shell Programs" tells how to create, execute, and debug shell programs and also how to use the dot (`.`) command. This section also includes examples of useful shell programs and programming hints.

Finally, the "Related UNIX Commands" section contains brief descriptions of UNIX commands that are helpful when writing shell programs.

Special Notations

Information applicable to only the Korn shell is indicated with the notation *KSH only,* with the text boxed and screened as follows:

KSH only
> *KSH only* information does not apply to the Bourne shell.

The value that the command returns to the shell on completion is noted, where applicable, with the notation *Return Value*.

Conventions

The following conventions are used throughout this book:

- Commands (including built-in shell commands, UNIX commands, and programming constructs) are shown in **boldface** type.

- Names of files, directories, and command options are shown in *italics*.

- Names of predefined shell variables and parameters are shown in *UPPERCASE ITALICS*.

- Special shell metacharacters, output from a command, and shell examples are shown in `monospace` font.

- A number in parentheses, such as (1), indicates a UNIX command. A description of the command is in the corresponding section of the following reference manuals:

Manual	*Section(s) Covered*
User's Reference Manual	1
Programmer's Reference Manual	2, 3, 4, and 7
System Administrator's Reference Manual	1M, 7, and 8

- The notation Ctrl-x indicates a control character that you enter by pressing the Ctrl key and the x key at the same time.

- The notation Esc-x indicates an escape sequence. Press the Esc key and release it, and then press x.

SHELL BASICS

Commands

Simple Commands

A *simple* command is a sequence of *words* separated by blanks (spaces or tabs). The first word is usually the name of a UNIX command or a built-in shell command. Additional words are either the name of files to be processed or arguments that modify the command's behavior.

A simple command returns an exit status if it terminates normally. For normal termination, the exit status is zero (0) if the command is successful, non-zero if unsuccessful. In the shell a zero indicates *true*, a non-zero indicates *false*.

If a command terminates abnormally, it returns octal 200+*status*. Status is the value of the signal that caused the abnormal termination. For example, if the Del key is pressed to interrupt a command, the return value will be 130 (200 octal = 128 decimal + 02, the value of the interrupt signal). See signal (2) for a complete list of signals and their values.

A *pipeline* consists of one or more simple commands separated by the pipe symbol (|). The output of each command is sent to the input of the next command in the pipeline. Each command is executed as a separate process. After the last command exits, the shell returns to the user. The exit status of a pipeline is the exit status of the last command in the pipeline.

Sequential Commands

A *sequential* command list consists of one or more simple commands (or pipelines) separated by a semicolon (;), ampersand (&), double ampersand (&&), or double pipe symbol (| |). If used in a command list, these separators are evaluated from left to right with the following precedence:

- `&&` and `¦`
- `;` `&`

KSH only

A `¦&` may be used as a command terminator and has equal precedence with `;` and `&` (see "Co-Processes").

A semicolon causes sequential execution of the list of commands. The shell waits for each command in the list to complete before executing the next command. The output of each command is sent to the standard output. *Newlines* may be used in place of semicolons to delimit commands.

Commands separated by an ampersand (`&`) are executed asynchronously. The shell starts each command without waiting for the preceding command to complete execution.

A double ampersand (`&&`) causes the command following it to be executed only if the preceding command returns a 0 exit status. In the following example, the message `You have mail` is **echo**ed only if the **mail -s** command returns a 0 exit status:

```
mail -s && echo You have mail
```

The double pipe symbol (`¦¦`) causes the command that follows it to be executed only if the preceding command returns a non-zero exit status. In the next example, the message `No mail` is **echo**ed if the **mail -s** command returns a non-zero:

```
mail -s ¦¦ echo No mail
```

KSH only

The `¦&` symbol used to separate commands in the **ksh** causes asynchronous execution of the preceding command or pipeline with a two-way pipe established to the parent shell. The standard I/O of the spawned command can be written to and read from by the parent shell by using the **-p** option to the **read** and **print** built-in commands. Only one asynchronous command can be active at any time.

Group Commands

You can group a sequential list of commands together by enclosing the commands in parentheses. Standard input can be redirected into the group, and the standard output of the entire group can be redirected. For example, in the following command:

```
$ ls;who;date > status
```

only the output of the **date** command is sent to the file *status*.

However, if the entire list is enclosed in parentheses:

```
$ (ls;who;date) > status
```

the output of all three commands is sent to the file *status*.

To run the entire group asynchronously in the background, you would use the following:

```
$ (ls;who;date) > status&
```

Command Substitution

The output of a command can be used as the input to another command or for variable assignment with command substitution.

Whenever the shell encounters a command enclosed in grave accents, that command is executed first and its output becomes the input to another command or variable assignment. For example:

```
$ here=`pwd`
```

first executes the **pwd** command and then assigns its output to the variable *here*. Similarly,

```
$ pg `cat list`
```

paginates (**pg**) the files contained in the file *list*.

Command substitution is very useful for setting positional parameters with the **set** command. The following command:

```
$ set `date`
$ echo $1
Wed
$ echo $2
Dec
$ echo $*
Wed Dec 27 09:21:29 EST 1989
```

sets the positional parameters $1 through $6 with the output of the **date** command. Thus, $1 contains the day (Wed), $2 the month (Dec), etc. **echo $*** prints all the positional parameters.

The command is executed in a subshell. Interpretation is not performed before the command is read, except that backslashes used to escape other characters are removed. Backslashes (\) may be used to escape a grave accent (`) or another backslash that is to be passed through to another command within the command substitution. For example,

```
$ echo `basename \`pwd\``
```
would print the current directory's *basename*.

If a backslash is used to escape a newline character, both the backslash and newline are removed. Backslashes used to escape a dollar sign (\$) are removed also. This has no effect because no interpretation is done on the command before it is read. Backslashes used to escape the meaning of other special characters (other than \, `, ", newline, and $) are left intact when the command is read.

KSH only

The notation $(*cmd*) can be used in place of `*cmd*`.

Comments -

The # is used to specify that all text following it up to a newline is a comment (to be ignored by the shell). Comments are useful within a shell program to document how the program works.

Blank Interpretation

After parameter and command substitution, the shell separates arguments according to the value of the internal field-separator variable *IFS*. By default, the *IFS* is set to space, tab, and newline. *Explicit* null arguments ("" and ' ') are retained; *implicit* null arguments (those resulting from parameters that have no value) are removed.

The value of *IFS* can be changed to modify the way the shell separates its arguments. For example, setting the *IFS* to a colon (:) allows the following command:

```
$ IFS=:
$ ls:-1
```

This method can be used to make the shell parse lines separated by characters other than spaces. In the following example:

```
$ grep bill /etc/passwd
bill:fXAdztStiQVIU:100:21:Book
    Author:\
/usr/bill:/bin/sh
$ IFS=:
$ set `grep bill /etc/passwd`
$ echo $1
bill
$ echo $5
Book Author
```

the shell separates the line from the /etc/passwd file into seven parameters determined by the current value of *IFS* (:). The command substitution used with the **set** command sets each of these seven fields into the positional parameters $1 through $7 (the shell uses the value of *IFS* to separate fields). Therefore, each field could then be addressed by its positional parameter value. Notice that spacing for the *description* field ($5) remained intact. Using this method, the shell can be used as a simple database management system.

The value of *IFS* should never be set to that of one of the special shell characters ($\star$, >, ; , etc.).

Quoting

In many instances, you must prevent the shell from interpolating the meaning of special characters such as *, ?, [ ], spaces, tabs, and so on. For example, you may need to pass a special character through the shell to another program such as **grep(1)**. To accomplish this, there are three ways of quoting to prevent the shell from interpolating special characters.

Single Quotation Marks

Anything enclosed in single quotation marks is passed through the shell intact; that is, the shell does not interpolate a string enclosed in single quotation marks. In the following example:

```
$ echo '$TERM'
$TERM
```

the shell will not interpolate the $ as the lead-in character for a variable value.

Double Quotation Marks

Double quotation marks prevent the shell from interpolating everything *except* the dollar sign ($), backslash (\), and grave accent (`) symbols. Double quotation marks are used also when spaces or tabs are included in a string. The shell interprets all other special characters.

In the following examples:

```
$ name="Tom Jones"  # Keep the space
                           intact.
$ echo $name
Tom Jones          # Two arguments to the
                   # echo command
$ echo "$name"      # One argument to
                         echo
Tom Jones
```

the double quotation marks prevent the shell from interpolating the spaces, thus providing only one argument to the second **echo** command.

Backslash

The \ not only prevents the shell from interpolating the character immediately following it, but also prevents interpretation of spaces, tabs, and the newline character. The following example shows how the \ is used:

```
$ echo *
chapt01 chapt02 chapt03
$ echo \*
*
```

File-name Generation

Certain characters, often called *wild cards* or *shell metacharacters*, have special meaning to the shell.

Before a command is executed, the shell scans the command line for the following special file-name generation characters:

Character	*Meaning*
*	Match anything, including null string
?	Match any single character
[. . .]	Match any single character enclosed in brackets

If one of these characters is present, it is regarded as a special pattern-matching character; the shell attempts to generate a list of file names that match the meaning of the special character. If the shell finds no file names that match the pattern, the special character is left intact.

To specify a range of characters, use a – to separate the characters enclosed in brackets. For example, [a-z] will match any single character in the range of a through z. If the first character following the opening bracket is an exclamation mark, as in [!, any character not enclosed in the brackets is matched.

Tilde Substitution

KSH only

The **ksh** checks each word of an alias substitution to see whether it begins with a tilde (~). If it does, the word (up to a /) is checked to see whether it matches one of the following characters:

Character	Meaning
~	Replace tilde with value of *HOME*.
~+	Replace word (up to /) with value of *PWD*.
~-	Replace word (up to /) with value of *OLDPWD*.
~login	Replace tilde with a home directory that matches *login* name. If *login* name is not a valid user on this system, no replacement occurs.

A tilde followed by anything else is left unchanged.

If, in the value of a variable assignment, a tilde follows the equal sign, the **ksh** attempts tilde expansion using the preceding rules.

Invocation

When a user logs in, **login(1)** starts a shell process. A – is prepended to the name of the login shell process (**-sh**) and this shell initially reads commands from the files `/etc/profile` and `$HOME/.profile`, if they exist.

KSH only

If the *ENV* variable is set, its value is used as the environment file name and this file is read whenever a new **ksh** process is invoked, either directly or as a subshell. Thus, functions, parameters, and other shell constructs set within this file are available to all **ksh** subshells.

Following invocation, the shell reads commands as described in the following table. The first argument is assumed to be the name of a file containing commands; the remaining arguments are passed as positional parameters to that command file, unless the **-c** or **-s** options are specified.

Option	*Meaning*
-c *string*	If **-c** option is present, commands are read from *string*.
-s	If **-s** option is present or if no arguments remain, commands are read from standard input. Any remaining arguments specify the positional parameters. Shell output (except as described under "Built-In Commands") is written to file descriptor 2.
-i	If **-i** option is present or if shell input and output are attached to a terminal, the shell is *interactive*. In this case, the TERMINATE signal is ignored (so that **kill 0** does not kill an interactive shell) and the INTERRUPT signal is caught and ignored (so that **wait** is interruptible). In all cases, the shell ignores the QUIT signal. (See the "Signals" section for further discussion of TERMINATE, INTERRUPT, and QUIT.)
-r	If **-r** option is present, the shell is a restricted shell.

For descriptions of the remaining options and arguments, see the **set** command.

Arithmetic Operations

KSH only

The **let** command in the **ksh** provides integer arithmetic operations using long arithmetic. You can represent a named variable internally by using the **typeset -i** command, as in the following example:

```
# Declare num as a integer variable
typeset -i num
```

A base between 2 and 36 may be specified with the
typeset -i command to represent the notation the number
should take, as in:

```
# Declare binary as a base 2 integer
typeset -i2 binary
```

You can provide arithmetic functions on declared
integer variables by using the **let** command, as in the
following example:

```
$ typeset -i num1 num2 ans
$ num1=5
$ num2=8
$ let ans="$num1 + $num2"
$ print $ans
13
```

Many of the arithmetic operators for the **let** command
(*, <, >, etc.) require quoting to prevent the shell from
interpreting them.

The notation ((. . .)) can be used in place of the
let command. For example, the following can be used in
place of the previous example:

```
$ ((ans = $num1 * $num2))
$ print $ans
40
```

Prompting

The shell variable *PS1* (default $) is used as the primary
prompt sign and is printed before the shell reads each
command. If the shell requires additional information to
complete the command, it will prompt with the
secondary prompt sign *PS2* (default >).

Signals

A subshell inherits the signal values from its parent except that the INTERRUPT and QUIT signals for a command are ignored if the command is executed in the background (followed by an &). For more information and a list of signals used by the shell, see the **trap** command.

Execution

The shell executes commands as follows:

1. First, file-name generation, quoting, command substitution, variable substitution, and I/O redirection are resolved.

2. Built-in commands are first executed within the current shell.

3. The command name is then compared to names of the defined functions. If a match is found, the function is executed in current shell process with positional parameters (*$1*, *$2*, etc.) set as arguments to the function.

4. If a command is neither a built-in command nor a function, a new process is created and the shell attempts to execute the command via the system call *exec(2)*.

The shell uses the value of the *PATH* parameter to search for commands. The default value of *PATH*

```
:/bin:/usr/bin
```

specifies to search the current directory, then /bin, and then /usr/bin. The current directory is specified by a null path name or a dot (.) and can appear immediately after the = sign, between two colon delimiters, or at the end of the list. The following examples show how to set the current directory in the *PATH* parameter:

```
# Search current directory first
PATH=:/bin:/usr/bin
# Search current directory second
PATH=/bin::/usr/bin
# Search current directory last
PATH=/bin:/usr/bin:
# Do not search current directory
PATH=/bin:/usr/bin
```

For security purposes, system directories
(/bin, /usr/bin, etc.) should always be searched
first, before local directories or the current directory.

If a command contains a /, the search path is not used.
If the command begins with a /, it is an absolute path
name; otherwise, the path name is relative to the current
directory. Commands containing a / cannot be executed
from the restricted shell (/bin/rsh).

If, in the search path, the shell finds a file with the
command name that has execute permissions set but is
not an a.out file (one that contains directly executable
code), it is assumed to be a file containing shell
commands. A subshell is spawned to read and execute
the commands within the file.

The shell remembers the search path of each command it
executes to help avoid unnecessary *exec* system calls.
However, the location of a command found in a relative
directory must be redetermined whenever the relative
directory changes. The shell forgets all remembered
locations whenever the **hash -r** command (see "Built-In
Commands") is executed or when the *PATH* parameter
changes.

Shell Exit Status

The shell normally returns the exit status of the last
command executed or the value specified by the **exit**
built-in command. If the shell detects an error, it will
return a non-zero exit status. If the shell detects an error
while executing a shell script, execution terminates
immediately and a non-zero exit status is returned. The
exit status is available in the special shell variable *$?*.

Background Processing

A command can be run in the *background* instead of interactively. When a command is run in the background, the shell immediately returns a prompt to the user. The user can continue interactive use of the shell or start additional background commands.

To start a background command, append an ampersand (`&`) to the command line as follows:

```
$ sort large_file > file.out&
1222
```

A command started in the background becomes detached from the user's terminal. The standard input is redirected from `/dev/null` instead of the user's terminal. Because the `INTERRUPT` and `QUIT` signals are disabled, the Break and Del (delete) keys cannot be used to terminate the job. However, the `HANGUP` signal will still be sent to any background jobs when the login shell terminates.

Standard output and standard error are still redirected to the user's terminal when background jobs are executed. The standard output and standard error should be redirected to a file, if necessary, so that output from the background job does not interfere with output from interactive jobs (see "I/O Redirection").

When a background job is started, its process id (**PID**) is printed before the shell issues another prompt. The **ps** command can be used to determine the **PID** of any background jobs.

To terminate a background job, the **kill** command is used as follows:

```
$ kill -2 1222
```

In this example, `-2` is the signal to be sent (see "Signals") and `1222` is the background job's **PID**.

To make a background command immune to the hangup signal (`-1`), use the **nohup** (no hangup) command. **Nohup** is often used when a user wants to start a job and then log off. The following example shows how to start a job with **nohup**:

```
$ nohup sort database> db.out&
1245
```

The **wait** command can be used to wait on a background process and obtain its exit status. An optional argument (the **PID** of the job to be waited for) may be supplied to **wait**; however, if the **PID** does not exist, all background jobs are waited for and the exit status is set to 0.

To wait for a job with **PID** 1245, for example, enter the following command:

```
$ wait 1245
```

If a **wait** command is entered, the Break and Del keys send INTERRUPT and QUIT signals to the **wait** command instead of to the process being waited for.

A limit is set on the number of processes (commands) that each user can start. If this limit is exceeded, the error message cannot fork, too many processes is printed.

Job Control Mechanism

KSH only

An interactive **ksh** associates a job with each command if the **set -o monitor** option is turned on. The **jobs** command will print a list of currently running jobs. When a job is started in the background with &, the shell prints a line similar to the following:

```
$ sort largedata > sort.out&
[1] 1923
```

In the preceding line, [1] indicates that this is job number 1; 1923, that one process is associated with it.

To refer to a job, use the character %. Combine it with an integer (%1, for example, to refer to job number 1) or with a string indicating the first part of a command name (%so to refer to the last job that started with **so**).

The notations %+ and %- refer to the current and preceding jobs, respectively. A %% refers to the current job.

When a process state changes, the shell is notified immediately. Prior to a prompt, the shell notifies the user when a job becomes blocked and cannot continue. Thus, the shell does not interrupt the user's work.

When a user tries to exit a shell in which background jobs are active (running or stopped), the message `You have running(stopped) jobs` is displayed. If, after using the **jobs** command to see what the jobs are, the user immediately tries to exit, the shell does not repeat the warning and all background jobs are killed. Use the **nohup(1)** command to prevent jobs from being terminated when a user exits the shell.

On systems with hardware that supports job control, certain features of the shell provide more precise control of jobs. Pressing Ctrl-Z (^Z) sends a `STOP` signal to the current job. The shell stops the job, prints `Stopped`, and prints another prompt. You can put the job into the background by using the **bg** built-in command; a background job, either running or stopped, can be brought into the foreground with the **fg** built-in command. A ^Z takes effect immediately. Pending output and unread input are discarded.

Background jobs will stop if they attempt to read input from the terminal, but normally can send output to the terminal. To prevent output from background jobs, issue the **stty tostop** command. With this tty option set, background jobs will stop when they try to produce output as they do when they try to read input.

Co-Processes

KSH only

In the **ksh**, two processes can be started that can communicate with each other. The concept is simple: one shell program starts another (using the `|&` operator) and then, using the **print -p** and **read -p** commands, information can be exchanged between the two processes. The process that is started, called a *co-process*, must do the following:

- Send all output to the standard output

- Place a newline character at the end of each message

- Flush its standard output at the end of each message

The following two programs illustrate the use of co-processes. The first program, the co-process, returns the sum of two numbers passed to it:

```
# Program: sum - add two numbers
while true
do
read a b
let ans="$a + $b"
print  $ans
done
```

The second program, the main process, starts **sum** and then prompts the user for two numbers. It passes the two numbers to **sum**, receives the answer, and prints it on the terminal.

```
# Program: query
sum |&  # Start-p sum
while true
do
# Ask for the first number
print "Enter num1"
read num1
# Ask for the second number
print "Enter num2"
read num2
# Pass the numbers to sum
print -p $num1 $num2
# Get the answer
read -p ans
# Print it on the terminal
print "Sum of $num1 + $num2 = $ans"
done
```

The co-process (**sum**) continues to run until the main process (**query**) dies.

Using co-processes, you can develop transaction-oriented shell programs for database applications and so on.

In **ksh** versions newer than that of 06/03/86, multiple co-processes may be started. Each co-process (after the first) must be assigned a unique file descriptor for its input and output. To assign standard output for a co-process, use the notation **exec 3>&p**; to reassign the standard input, use **exec 3<&p**.

Within a co-process, output must be redirected to the file descriptor associated with the co-process. For example, **print $ans >&3** sends output of the **print** command to file descriptor number 3.

The main process would use **print -pu4 num1**, for example, to send output to the co-process associated with file descriptor number 4, and **read -pu4** to receive input from co-process number 4.

The following programs illustrate the use of more than one co-process. Two co-processes, **add** and **subtract**, are started:

Co-Process 1:

```
# Program: add
while true
do
read a b
let ans="$a + $b"
print  $ans
done
```

Co-Process 2:

```
while true
do
read a b
let ans="$a - $b"
print -r $ans >&4
done
```

In the main program (**query**), which follows, file descriptor 4 is associated with **add**, and file descriptor 5 is associated with **subtract**. The program uses a **select** statement to determine which co-process to write to and read from.

```
# Program: query (2 co-processes)
PS3="Choose function: "
# Start up add co-process
add |&
# Move to file desc. 4
exec 4>&p
# Start-up subtract co-process
subtract |&
# Move to file desc. 5
exec 5>&p
while true
do
# Get 1st number
print "Enter num1"
read num1
# Get 2nd number
print "Enter num2"
read num2
# Select function to perform
select F in add subtract quit
do
    case $REPLY
    in
      1)
          # Write to add
          print -ru4 $num1 $num2
          # Read from add
          read -ru4 ans
          break ;;
      2)
          # Write to subtract
          print -ru5 $num1 $num2
          # Read from subtract
          read -ru5 ans
          break ;;
      3)
          exit ;;
    esac
done
# Print the answer
print "Answer = $ans"
done
```

Reentering Commands

KSH only

When a command is executed, the text of the command is appended, by default, to a file named $HOME/.history. You can set the variable *HISTFILE* to change the name of this history file. The variable *HISTSIZE* (default 128) is used to set the number of commands of which **ksh** will maintain a history.

The **fc -l** command can be used to list all or part of the *HISTFILE*. To list only part of the file, you specify the first and last commands that you want listed, as in the following example:

```
# List the last 16 commands
$ fc -l
# List commands 2 through 12
$ fc -l 2 12
# Display the last 5 commands
$ fc -l -5
```

The command **r** (the **repeat** command, an alias of fc -e -) is used to reexecute a previous command from the *HISTFILE* file. By default, with no arguments, **r** reexecutes the last command. You can specify a command by a positive or negative number, or by a partial string containing the first few letters of the command to be reexecuted, as in the following example:

```
# Repeat the last command
$ r
ls -l
# Repeat command number 8
$ r 8
who
# Repeat the 4th command back
$ r -4
ps
# Repeat the last command starting
# with an "l"
$ r l
ls -l
```

Command-line Editing

KSH only

The **ksh** supports command-line editing using either the **emacs** or **vi** editor. **emacs** is provided in two versions, **emacs** and **gmacs**. The only difference is when Ctrl-t is pressed: **emacs** transposes the current character with the next character, and **gmacs** transposes the two previous characters.

To use the command-line editing features, you must set one of the following **ksh** options: **emacs**, **gmacs**, or **vi**. An example of such a setting is **set -o vi**. If the value of either the *VISUAL* or *EDITOR* variables ends in **emacs**, **gmacs**, or **vi**, the corresponding **ksh** option is set automatically to that editor.

The value of the variable *FCEDIT* is used to select which editor to use with the **fc** command. If *FCEDIT* is not set, /bin/ed is used as the default editor.

The **fc** (**fix command**) is used to invoke the command-line editing feature. Enter **fc** alone to invoke the editor (*FCEDIT*) on the last command stored in the *HISTFILE*. Enter **fc** with a number to invoke the editor on that number command from the *HISTFILE*. If the first and last options are specified to the **fc** command, the editor is invoked for that list of commands:

```
# Edit commands 5 thru 10
$ fc 5 10
```

In the preceding example, the first command is the fifth command and the last command is command 10. If a string is given, **fc** invokes the editor on the last command that starts with the string, as in:

```
# Edit a command starting with w
$ fc w
```

On exiting the editor, the edited command(s) are printed and reexecuted.

If the name of the editor to the **fc -e** command is a **-**, as in the following example:

```
# Repeat the last command
$ fc -e -
```

then editing is skipped; the first command is reexecuted directly.

This form of the command also accepts substitutions such as `old=new`. Because **fc -e -** is aliased as **r**, the command:

```
$ r bin=usr ls
```

substitutes *usr* for *bin* in the last **ls** command.

To invoke the command-line editing feature, enter the appropriate `fetch previous command` sequence: press Esc-k for **vi** or Ctrl-P in **emacs** or **gmacs**. Other **fetch** commands can be entered to recall specific command lines (see the appropriate editing mode summaries later in this section).

A command that has been fetched is displayed in a single-line window of *COLUMNS* wide. If the variable *COLUMNS* is not set, the window is 80 columns wide. If a line is longer than the value of *COLUMNS* minus 2, a mark at the end of the line indicates that additional text follows. As the cursor moves and reaches the window's boundaries, the window is centered on the cursor. The marks >, <, and * indicate that the line extends to the right, left, or both sides of the window, respectively.

The editing commands shown for **emacs** and **vi** modes in the following sections can be used within the window, depending on the editor selected by the **set -o** option. A RETURN or LINE FEED indicates the end of the editing mode; then the modified command line is executed.

emacs Editing Mode

To set **emacs** editing mode, enter the following:

```
set -o emacs
set -o gmacs
```

The only difference between **emacs** and **gmacs** modes is the way Ctrl-t is handled (see the table of **emacs** commands in this section).

To edit a command line, first recall it by using a **fetch** command (Ctrl-p) and then move the cursor to the point needing correction. Insert or delete characters or words as necessary.

All editing commands consist either of control characters or escape sequences. Control characters are notated by Ctrl- followed by a character. For example, Ctrl-x is the notation for pressing Ctrl key and the x character key at the same time. Do not press the Shift key (although control sequences are indicated with capital letters).

Del indicates that the delete key should be pressed.

Escape sequences are shown as Esc- followed by a character. For example, you enter Esc-d by pressing the Esc key, releasing it, and then pressing the d key. Esc-x indicates that you should press Esc and then x.

The following **emacs** commands are implemented in the **ksh**:

Command	_Meaning_
Ctrl-f	Move cursor forward one character
Esc-f	Move cursor forward one word
Ctrl-b	Move cursor back one character
Esc-b	Move cursor back one word
Ctrl-a	Move cursor to start of line
Ctrl-e	Move cursor to end of line
Ctrl-]x	Move cursor to character x on current line
Ctrl-xCtrl-x	Transpose the cursor and the mark
Ctrl-h	Delete preceding character
Ctrl-d	Delete current character
Esc-d	Delete current word
Esc-Ctrl-h	Delete preceding word
Esc-h	Delete preceding word

Command	*Meaning*
Esc-Del	Delete preceding word. If the interrupt character is Del, this command will not work.
Ctrl-t	In **emacs** mode, transpose current character with next character. In **gmacs** mode, transpose two preceding characters.
Ctrl-c	Capitalize current character
Esc-c	Capitalize current word
Ctrl-k	Delete from cursor to end of line. If given a parameter of zero, delete from start of line to cursor.
Ctrl-w	Delete from cursor to mark
Esc-p	Push region from cursor to mark on the stack
Ctrl-g	Kill entire current line. If 2 kill characters are entered in succession, all subsequent kill characters cause a line feed. (This is useful when using hard-copy terminals.)
Ctrl-y	Restore last item removed from line
Ctrl-l	Line feed and print current line
Ctrl-@	Set mark
Esc-space	Set mark
Ctrl-j	Execute current line
Ctrl-m	Execute current line
Ctrl-d	Terminate shell if current line is null
Ctrl-p	Fetch previous command. Whenever Ctrl-p is pressed, retrieve preceding command from *HISTFILE*.
Esc-<	Fetch least recent history line
Esc->	Fetch most recent history line
Ctrl-n	Fetch next command. Whenever Ctrl-n is pressed, retrieve next command in *HISTFILE*.

Command	*Meaning*
Ctrl-r*string*	Reverse search history for a previous command line containing *string*. If a parameter of zero is given, search is forward. *string* is terminated by a `return` or `newline` character.
Ctrl-o	Execute current line and fetch next line relative to current line from the *HISTFILE*
Esc-*num*	Define numeric parameter. The *num* is taken as a parameter to the next command. Commands that accept a parameter are Ctrl-f, Ctrl-b, Ctrl-d, Ctrl-k, Ctrl-r, Ctrl-p, Ctrl-n, and Del.
Esc-*letter*	Search alias list for the name _*letter*. If an alias of this name is defined, its value is inserted on the line. The *letter* must not be one of the preceding escape sequences.
Esc-_	Insert last parameter of preceding command on the line
Esc-.	Insert last parameter of preceding command on the line
Esc-*	Attempt file-name generation on current word
Ctrl-u	Multiply parameter of next command by 4
\	Escape special meaning of next character.
	Edit characters and erase, kill, and interrupt characters may be entered in a command line or in a search string if preceded by a \.
Ctrl-v	Display version of shell

vi Editing Mode

To set **vi** editing mode, enter the following command:

```
set -o vi
```

The **viraw** option may also be set to specify character-at-a-time input. This mode is often set for terminals operating at 1200 baud or less and those that do not support two alternate end-of-line delimiters.

Next, you can edit a command line by fetching it into the edit window with an Esc-k command. Then the cursor is moved to the appropriate place in the editing window, and characters or words are inserted or deleted as necessary. When a `return` or `newline` character is entered, the edited command is executed.

The following command sections summarize the **vi** editor commands built into **ksh**. Most escape sequences accept an optional repeat *count* prior to the command.

Input Commands:

Command	*Meaning*
Ctrl-h	Delete preceding character
Ctrl-w	Delete preceding word
Ctrl-d	Terminate shell
Ctrl-v	Escape character immediately following Ctrl-v
\	Escape next *erase* or *kill* character

Cursor Commands:

Command	*Meaning*
[*count*]**l**	Move cursor forward one character
[*count*]**w**	Move cursor forward one word
[*count*]**W**	Move cursor to beginning of next word that follows a blank
[*count*]**e**	Move cursor to end of word
[*count*]**E**	Move cursor to end of current word
[*count*]**h**	Move cursor back one character
[*count*]**b**	Move cursor back one word
[*count*]**B**	Move cursor to preceding blank separated word

Cursor Commands:

Command	Meaning
[*count*]f*x*	Find next character *x* in current line
[*count*]F*x*	Find previous character *x* in current line
[*count*]t*x*	Move cursor to next character *x*
[*count*]T*x*	Move cursor to preceding character *x*
;	Repeat last single-character **find** command (**f**, **F**, **t**, or **T**)
,	Reverse last single-character **find** command
0	Move cursor to start of line
^	Move cursor to first nonblank character in line
$	Move cursor to end of line

Search Commands:

Command	Meaning
[*count*]k	Fetch previous command. Whenever **k** is entered, retrieve previous command from *HISTFILE*
[*count*]-	Equivalent to **k**
[*count*]j	Fetch next command. Whenever **j** is entered, next command from *HISTFILE* is retrieved.
[*count*]+	Equivalent to **j**
[*count*]G	Fetch command number *count*
/*regexp*	Search backward through history for a previous command containing the regular expression *regexp*. If *regexp* is null, the preceding search pattern is used. *regexp* is terminated by a return or newline character.
?*regexp*	Same as / (except that search is forward)

Search Commands:

Command	Meaning
n	Search for next match of last pattern to **/** or **?** commands
N	Search for next match of last pattern to **/** or **?**, but in reverse direction

Text Modification Commands:

Command	Meaning
a	Enter input mode and enter text after the current character
A	Append text to end of line. Same as **$a**.
[*count*]**c***dir* **c**[*count*]*dir*	Delete current character through character *dir*, where *dir* is a cursor-movement command; then enter input mode. If *dir* is **c**, entire line is deleted and input mode is entered.
C	Delete current character through end of line and enter input mode (same as **c$**)
S	Equivalent to **cc**
D	Delete current character through end of line
d[*count*]*dir* [*count*]**d***dir*	Delete current character to which character *dir* moves the cursor. Same as **d$**. If *dir* is **d**, entire line is deleted.
i	Enter input mode and insert text before current character
I	Insert text before beginning of line. Equivalent to two-character sequence **^i**.
[*count*]**P**	Place preceding text modification before cursor
[*count*]**p**	Place preceding text modification after cursor
R	Enter input mode and overlay characters on screen with characters you type
r*c*	Replace current character with *c*

Text Modification Commands:

Command	Meaning
[count]x	Delete current character
[count]X	Delete preceding character
[count].	Repeat preceding text-modification command
~	Toggle (or change) the case of current character and advance cursor
[count]_	Append the *count* word of preceding command and enter the input mode. The last word is used if *count* is omitted.
*	Append an * to the current word and attempt file name generation. If no match is found, the bell is rung; otherwise, the word is replaced by matching pattern and the input mode is entered.

Miscellaneous Commands:

Command	Meaning
u	Undo last text-modifying command
U	Undo all text-modifying command performed on the line
[count]v	Returns the command fc -e ${VISUAL:-${EDITOR:-vi}} *count* in the input buffer. If *count* is omitted, current line is used.
Ctrl-l	Line feed and print current line. Has effect only in control mode.
Ctrl-j	Execute current line, regardless of mode
Ctrl-m	Execute current line, regardless of mode
#	Equivalent to I#<cr>. Useful for causing current line to be inserted in history without being executed.

I/O Redirection

On UNIX, all input/output is performed through files. When a shell command is executed, three files are opened automatically and associated with the command:

File Descriptor	*Name*	*Description*
0	stdin	Keyboard
1	stdout	Terminal
2	stderr	Terminal

All commands normally accept input from stdin (keyboard). Normal output is sent to stdout (terminal). Error messages are sent to stderr (terminal).

You can redirect input and output by using special notations that the shell interprets. The command line is scanned for these special characters; if any are found, the shell sets up redirection *before* the command is executed. When input or output is redirected, no file-name expansion occurs (in other words, use of the special characters *, ?, and [ ] is not allowed).

If a command is followed by &, the default standard input for that command is the empty file /dev/null. Otherwise, the environment for execution of a command contains the invoking shell's file descriptors as modified by input/output specifications.

The following notations are used to specify redirection; unless otherwise noted, spacing is not critical.

Notation	*Meaning*
<*file*	Use *file* as standard input (file descriptor 0)
>*file*	Use *file* as standard output (file descriptor 1). If *file* does not exist, it is created; otherwise, it is truncated to zero length.
>>*file*	Use *file* as standard output. If *file* exists, output is appended to it (by first seeking the end-of-file); otherwise, *file* is created.

Notation	*Meaning*
`<< [-] word`	Shell input is read up to a line that is the same as *word*, or to an end-of-file. The resulting document becomes the standard input. If any character of *word* is quoted (enclosed in quotation marks), no interpretation is placed on characters of document; otherwise, parameter command substitution occurs, escaped `newlines` are ignored, and a \ must be used to quote the characters \, $, and `.

– is appended to **<<** (no space allowed), and all leading tabs are stripped from *word* before shell input is read (but after parameter and command substitution is done on *word*). Leading tabs are stripped from shell input as it is read and before each line is compared with *word*. Shell input is read up to the first line that literally matches the resulting *word*, or to an end-of-file.

| `<&digit` | Standard input is duplicated from the file descriptor digit (see **dup**(2)). You can duplicate standard output similarly, by using > instead of <. Do not place spaces between the < and &; doing so causes the shell to interpret the syntax as a background command. |
| `<&-` | Standard input is closed. You can close standard output similarly by using > instead of <. Do not place spaces between the < and &. |

If `<&digit` or `<&-` is preceded by a digit, the file descriptor created is that specified by the digit (instead of the default 0 or 1). For example:

```
...  2>&1
```

creates file descriptor 2, which is a duplicate of file descriptor 1.

The order in which redirections are specified is significant because the shell evaluates redirections from left to right. For example:

```
sort large_data > outfile 2>&1
```

first associates file descriptor 1 with file *outfile*. It then associates file descriptor 2 with the file (*outfile*) associated with file descriptor 1. If the order of redirections were reversed, file descriptor 2 would be associated with the terminal (assuming file descriptor 1 had been) and file descriptor 1 would be associated with the file *outfile*.

If a command is composed of several *simple* commands, redirection is evaluated for the entire command before it is evaluated for each *simple* command. The shell evaluates redirection in the following order:

1. for the entire command list

2. for each pipeline within the list

3. for each command within each pipeline

4. for each list within each command

The following examples illustrate these evaluation rules:

```
# Output from only the date command
# is redirected to file status:
$ who ; ls ; date > status
# Output from the entire list (group)
# is redirected to file status:
$ (who ; ls ; date) > status
# Output from the entire list (group)
# is redirected to the sort command:
$ (grep FL database ; grep MA
  database) | sort
```

Redirection of output is not allowed in the restricted shell.

Environment

Whenever a shell (login shell included) is invoked, a list of name-value pairs (called the *current environment*) is established for every parameter or variable. These name-value pairs are passed to an executed program in the same way a normal argument list is passed. If the user or a program modifies the value of any of these parameters or creates new parameters, they become part of the current environment. The **unset** command can remove a parameter from the current environment.

A variable or parameter must be exported (with the **export** command) before it can be accessed by subshells or commands invoked by the current shell. Any parameters modified by a subshell remain unchanged in the parent shell, whether or not they have been exported in the subshell. In other words, only exported parameters are available to subsequent shells.

The environment passed to a subshell or command is composed of any unmodified name-value pairs that have been exported minus those removed by the **unset** command.

To set parameter values for the login shell, place them in a file named `.profile` in the user's home directory. The shell reads this file upon login, establishing the user's login environment from name-value pairs found in the file. Changes made to this file will not take effect until the user logs in again or until the dot (.) command is used to read the file into the current shell:

```
. .profile
```

To modify the environment for a simple command, prefix it with one or more parameter assignments (provided that it is an exported parameter) as in the following example:

```
$ DIR=/tmp echo $DIR
/tmp
```

The **-k** option to the shell causes *all* keyword arguments to be placed in the current environment, regardless of their position in the command line. Notice the results of the following two commands:

```
$ export name
$ echo name=tom $name
name=tom
$ set -k
$ echo name=tom $name
tom
```

The first command, **echo name=tom $name**, was interpreted as a echo of the string *name=tom* and the variable *$name*. Because *$name* was not set, only the string *name=tom* was echoed.

After the command **set -k**, the shell placed the variable assignment *name=tom* in the current environment even though it occurred in the middle of the **echo** command. Thus, *tom* was printed as a result of the **echo** command.

Restricted Shell

The **rsh** is used to restrict the actions of the shell as follows:

- Changing directories is not allowed.

- The value of the *PATH* variable cannot be changed.

- Commands or paths containing a / cannot be executed or used.

- Output redirection (> and >>) is not allowed.

These restrictions are enforced after the login shell reads the `.profile` file.

A restricted shell is invoked as follows:

1. Specify `/bin/rsh` as the login shell in the `/etc/passwd` file. The environment variable *SHELL* is set; it has a value of `rsh` as the file name.

2. Use `/bin/rsh` or **rsh** to invoke a command.

3. Invoke the shell with the **-r** option.

Because **rsh** invokes **sh** to execute shell scripts, it is possible to give users the full power of the standard shell while limiting the commands they can execute. In other words, the system administrator sets up a directory of shell scripts that can be searched for and executed only by means of the **rsh**.

Normally, use of the restricted shell assumes that the user is placed in a separate subdirectory (normally not the login directory) and does not have both write and execute permissions in the same directory. By setting the *PATH* variable, working directory, and permissions, the creator of the user's `.profile` file has full control over which actions the user may perform.

Shell Security Features

UNIX System V.3 and later releases provide an enhanced Bourne shell that contains some additional security features, which are described in this section. To determine whether you have the enhanced version of the shell, enter the following command:

```
$ what /bin/sh
```

If you are running the enhanced shell, you will receive the message `/usr/adm/sh.sec.sl`.

The enhanced shell resets the effective user or group id when one or more of the following is true:

- The real and effective user id are not equal
- The real and effective group id are not equal
- The effective user id or group id is less than 100 (excluding group id 1)

These enhancements help prevent executing suid shells which may give a user unauthorized root privileges.

KSH only

The following additional security features are implemented in the **ksh**:

- The value of the *IFS* variable is reset to the default value when a shell script is invoked. It can only be set for the **read** built-in command and after parameter and command substitution. In other words, *IFS* cannot be changed for an interactive shell (for example, the login shell).

- Whenever the real and effective uid of a shell program are different, **ksh** goes into a *protected* mode. In this mode, the *PATH* variable is reset to a default value and the `.profile` and *ENV* files are not processed. Instead, the file `/etc/suid_profile` is read and executed. This gives an administrator control over the environment to set the *PATH* variable or to log setuid shell invocations. Security of the system is compromised if **/etc** or the file `/etc/suid_profile` is writable by all.

- The setuid root program **/etc/suid_exec** authenticates all requests to **exec** any shell scripts that cannot be opened for reading and that have their suid and/or setgid bits set. The program authenticates the request and **exec**s a shell with the correct bits set to carry out the task. This shell is invoked with the requested file already open for reading. For security reasons, this program is given the full pathname **/etc/suid_exec** in **/bin/ksh**.

Shell Notes

1. Special shell metacharacters used within I/O redirection constructs will not be interpreted. For example, `ls -l > l*` will create a file named `l*`.

2. Variables set in a pipeline have no effect on the parent shell because commands in a pipeline are run as separate processes.

3. If the current directory or its parent directory (the one above it) is removed, **pwd** may not give the correct responses. Use **cd** with a full path name to correct this problem.

4. In a pipeline with three or more stages, not all processes are children of the invoking shell and therefore cannot be waited for.

5. If *n* is not an active process id of a **wait** *n* command, all the shell's currently active background processes are waited for and the exit status is zero.

SHELL FILES AND PROCESSES

The UNIX file and process implementation method is what makes the shell so powerful. Because the shell can take advantage of both the UNIX file system and process control mechanism, an understanding of how these work will help you make the best use of the shell.

File System

The file system uses a hierarchical structure of files and directories to organize information. The file system starts at the root directory (/). Underneath the root directory are additional subdirectories. Each directory and subdirectory may contain files and directories. There is no limitation on the depth of a directory structure.

Naming Conventions

On System V UNIX, a directory or file name can consist of 14 characters. UNIX does not impose any file naming conventions, although upper- and lowercase characters in a file/directory name are distinct. A file/directory name should not contain any spaces, tabs, newlines, or characters which have special meaning to the shell (/, *, ;, etc.).

File names that begin with a . (dot) are not printed when the contents of a directory are listed with the **ls** command unless specifically requested by the **-a** option to **ls**.

A *pathname* is the name a command uses to locate a file or directory. An *absolute* pathname always begins with a / (slash) and contains all the components that tell where the file or directory is located. A *relative* pathname does not begin with a / and in this case the command will search for the file/directory in relation to the current directory.

The conventions . (dot) and .. (dot-dot) are used to refer to the current directory and parent directory, respectively. The parent directory is the directory immediately above the current directory. The parent directory of the root (/) directory is the root directory itself.

File Permissions

Access to each file and directory is controlled at three levels: the owner of the file, the members of a group that the file belongs to, or all other users on the system. These three accesses are referred to as *user*, *group*, and *other*.

When a file or directory is created, it is assigned the effective user id and effective group id of the person creating it. File access permissions can be assigned as follows:

- Read access for the user, group, and/or others

- Write access for the user, group, and/or others

- Execute permission for user, group, and/or others

- Set user id (suid) and/or set group id (sgid) permissions. If these permissions are set on an executable file, then when the program is executed, the effective user id and/or effective group id of the process being executed is set to the same as the user id and/or group id of the file that contains the program. (Note: suid and sgid permissions have no effect when executing shell scripts under the Bourne shell. The Korn shell has special security features built into it to control suid/sgid programs. See "Shell Security Features" in the "Shell Basics" section.)

- Set sticky bit. When this bit is set, an executable program is not removed from the swap device (if possible) when the program terminates. This makes the invocation of the program faster.

A directory may have the following permissions:

- Read permission for the user, group, and/or others. Read permission on a directory allows a user to list the contents of the directory.

- Write permission for the user, group, and/or others. Write permission on a directory allows a user to update the directory contents, which means that files and directories can be created, moved, and removed by any user who has write permission for that directory.

- Search permission for user, group, and/or others. With search permission set, the user may change directories into the directory.

- On some releases of UNIX, the sticky bit may be set on a directory. With this bit set, only the owner of the directory or the owner of a file in that directory may remove files in it.

The access permission of a file and directory is controlled by the user through the **chmod** command (see "Related UNIX Commands"). Each user can also establish a file creation mask that disables specified permissions when a new file or directory is created. The file creation mask is a three digit octal number set with the **umask** command. This number tells a process which permissions to "take away" when a new file/directory is created. For example, an **umask** value of **027** will remove write permission for the group and read/write/execute permissions for others. The initial file/directory access permissions are assigned as follows:

- For directories, the initial mode is **drwxrwxrwx** minus the user's **umask** value.

- For new files created by commands other than **cp**, the initial mode is `-rwxrwxrwx` minus the user's **umask** value.

- For new files created by the **cp** command, the permissions are the same as those of the source file. The **umask** value does not have any effect when files are created using the **cp** command.

File Descriptors

When the shell is first started it opens three files and associates each file with a number called a *file descriptor*. These three files are:

File Descriptor	*Name*	*Device*
0	Standard Input	Keyboard
1	Standard Output	CRT
2	Standard Error	CRT

File descriptor 0, the *standard input*, is initially opened for reading from the keyboard. File descriptor 1, the *standard output*, is initially opened for writing to the terminal CRT. File descriptor 2, the *standard error*, is initially opened for reading and writing. Error messages from most programs are written on the standard error to prevent their output from being mixed in with the normal output from a command.

When a program is invoked, it inherits these three file descriptors. Thus, each program reads from the standard input, writes to the standard output, and prints error messages on the standard error. If a program opens additional files, then they are assigned new file descriptors in sequence. By default, there is a limit of 20 open files per process on UNIX.

Special Files

UNIX accesses hardware devices through *special files*. These special files simply provide an interface between the operating system and a physical device such as a terminal or printer. These special files are normally kept in the */dev* directory.

Each terminal connected to UNIX is associated with a special file. To determine the name of the special device associated with your terminal, the **tty** command can be used. Through I/O redirection, the shell can read from and write to special files, if the file access permission is set correctly.

The special file */dev /null* is a zero-length special file that is often referred to as the "bit bucket." Unwanted output can be redirected to this file.

Processes

The UNIX system uses processes as a means of executing programs. Each command a user enters causes a *process* to be created. A process is a program in execution. In addition to the actual program itself, a process has associated with it information about the user and system environments. Each process has a unique *process id* associated with it that the operating system uses to distinguish it from other processes.

A process that creates another process is called a *parent* process. Any processes a parent creates are called *child* processes. A child process knows its parent through the *parent process id* (PPID).

A process also has associated with it a *process group id*. A process group consists of all processes with the same process group id. Each login shell can only have one process group id associated with it at a time. This is called the *foreground* process. If a user's process is not in the user's process group id that is associated with the user's login shell, then that process is a *background* process.

Also associated with each process are the real and effective user id, and the real and effective group id. The real user id and real group id are set by the login process and are inherited by all processes that the user creates. The effective user id is normally the same as the real user id but may be changed by programs that run as set user id (i.e., **su**). Likewise, the real and effective group ids are normally the same but the effective group id can be changed by programs that run as set group id (i.e., **mail**). The effective user id and effective group ids of a process are used to determine what permissions a process has for file/directory access (read, write, execute/search).

A process is created by either a **fork** or **exec** system call (a system call is a request a program makes to the operating system for system services).

fork System Call

A parent process creates a child process through the **fork** system call (see figure 1).

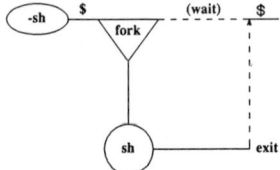

Fig. 1. Process creation.

A **fork** creates a copy of the original process that is identical to the parent process with the exception of its process id. The child process is given its own unique process id. The parent process may suspend its execution (wait) until the child process completes. Normally, the shell runs commands by creating child processes and then waiting for the child to complete before issuing another shell prompt to the user. The child process inherits the following environmental information from the parent:

- Parent process id
- Process group id
- Open files
- Working directory
- File creation mask (**umask**)
- Real and effective user ids
- Real and effective group ids
- File creation size limits
- Maximum memory limitations
- Signal setting actions
- Exported variables

Thus, a child process is initially identical to its parent. As the child process runs, it may modify its environment information. The parent process environment information is not affected by any changes the child process makes. For example, if the child process changes the value of a variable, the original value of the variable will still be in effect when the child exits.

When a process completes, control is returned to its parent. Any resources the process allocated are returned to the operating system for use by future processes. A child process also returns a number to its parent that indicates whether any errors occurred. This number is called the *return value* or *exit code*.

Normally, a return code of 0 indicates a success and a non-zero indicates an error.

exec System Call

An **exec** system call causes a process to overlay itself with the new process. The new process inherits all of the environment information of the process that issued the **exec**, including the process id. Thus, the only difference between **fork** and **exec** is the **exec**'d process has the same process id as the original process. When an **exec**'d process exits, it returns to the parent process associated with the parent process id that it inherited from the process which issued the **exec**.

Figure 2 shows the effect of the **exec** system call.

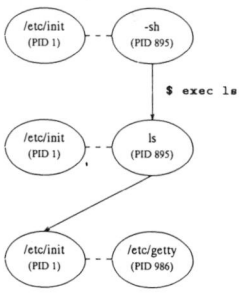

Fig. 2. exec *system call.*

The **-sh** was the login process and its parent was /etc/init. After the **exec ls** command was entered, the **-sh** process was overlayed with the **ls** process. Notice that the **ls** process inherits the process id (PID 895) of the **-sh** process. On completion of the **ls** command, control returned to the parent, /etc/init, which causes a login: prompt to be issued through /etc/getty.

The Login Process

The events that occur during login illustrate how the **fork** and **exec** system calls work. The /etc/init process (PID 1) is started during system start up and continues to run until the system is shut down. /etc/init is a system process and is not attached to a terminal. Processes of this nature are often called **deamons**.

/etc/init continually examines the */etc/inittab* file for work to be done. This file contains lines that tell /etc/init what commands it should execute for various system run levels and system events. Some lines in this file contain commands that print the login: prompt on each active terminal line. These lines are in the form of:

```
11:234:respawn:/etc/getty tty11 9600
```

This entry tells /etc/init to execute an /etc/getty command for tty11 at 9600 baud. The respawn indicates that each time the /etc/getty process dies it will be restarted by /etc/init.

Figure 3 shows the events that occur when a user logs in.

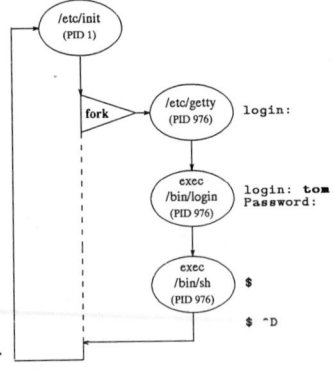

Fig. 3. Login process.

First, /etc/init **fork**s a /etc/getty process as indicated by the entry in */etc/inittab*. The /etc/getty process prints the login: message on the terminal. When a user enters his login name at the login: prompt, /etc/getty **exec**s /bin/login with the user's login name as an argument. /bin/login prompts the user for his password. After the user has entered his password, /bin/login validates the login name and password, and if both are correct, /bin/login **exec**s /bin/sh, which prints the $ shell prompt after it reads the system *letc/profile* and the user's *$HOME/profile* files.

The shell continues to run until the user logs out (with Ctrl-D or **exit**). When the shell terminates, it returns to its parent process. The parent process for the shell is /etc/init. Because the shell was invoked through a series of **fork** and **exec** system calls, it inherited the parent process id (PPID 1) and process id (PID 976) of the processes that invoked it.

Simple Command Execution

A simple command consists of any single UNIX or shell command and its arguments. When a simple command is entered, the shell **fork**s another shell and then an **exec** system call is made to execute the command. The parent shell waits until the child process has completed and then resumes control and issues another shell prompt. Figure 4 shows how an **ls** command would be executed.

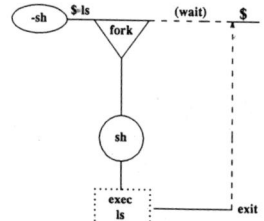

Fig. 4. Simple command execution.

Sequential Command Execution

A sequential command consists of two or more UNIX or shell commands separated by semicolons (;), as in ls;date. When a sequential command is entered, the shell **fork**s a subshell and then calls **exec** to execute the first command. When the first command completes, the shell **fork**s another shell and then calls **exec** to execute the second command. This sequence continues until all commands in the sequential command line are executed, as shown in figure 5.

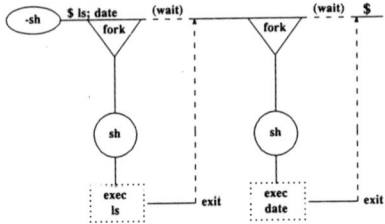

Fig. 5. Sequential command execution.

Notice that, on completion of each command in the sequential command line, control returns to the parent shell. Therefore, any environmental changes made by any command in the sequential command line will not affect subsequent commands. The return value to the parent shell is the return value of the last command in the sequential command line.

Group Command Execution

A group command consists of a sequential command enclosed in parentheses. Group commands are used when the output of all commands in the sequential command line are to be redirected to a file or sent to the input of another command via a pipe.

When a group command is entered, the shell **fork**s a subshell to execute the commands in the group (see figure 6).

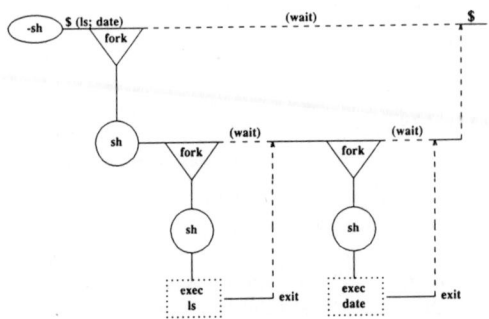

Fig. 6. Group command execution.

This subshell then **fork**s another shell which calls **exec** to execute the first command. On completion of the first command, another shell is **fork**ed which **exec**s the second command. This sequence continues until all the commands in the grouped sequential command line are executed. The return value from the group command is that of the last command in the group.

Pipe Command Execution

When the shell recognizes the pipe (|) special character in a command line, it starts up each process in the command line and establishes communications between them through a pipe special file. The last command in the pipe is started first, then the next to the last command, and so forth until all processes have been created (see figure 7).

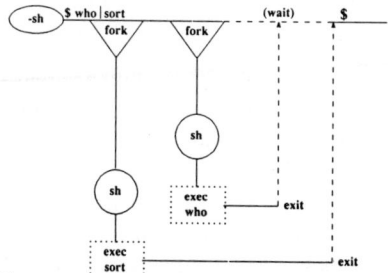

Fig. 7. Pipe.

Each process in the pipeline reads from its standard input and writes to its standard output. The standard input and standard output from each adjacent command is connected by a pipe special file. When a process attempts to read from a pipe it either

- Reads the data if another process has written to the pipe

- Suspends processing until another process writes data on the pipe

- Returns with an end-of-file indicator if no other process has the pipe open for writing

A process also can communicate with another process via signals. A child process also communicates with its parent by the exit status when it exits.

Background Command Exec.

Background command execution is invoked by following a UNIX or shell command with an ampersand (&). When a background command is entered, the shell **fork**s a subshell that **exec**s the command (see figure 8).

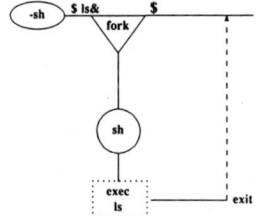

Fig. 8. Background command execution.

Control immediately returns to the parent shell, which issues another shell prompt ($). Additional UNIX or shell commands can then be executed in either the foreground or background.

Background jobs may also be entered sequentially or as a group. The following examples show various ways of entering background commands:

Example 1: Asynchronous Command Execution

The following shows how the **ls** and **date** commands can be executed asynchronously in the background.

```
$ ls & date &
```

Example 2. Group Background Command Execution

The following example shows how the **ls** and **date** commands can be executed in the background as a group.

```
$ (ls; date)&
```

Example 3: Asynchronous Group Command Execution

This example shows how two group commands can be executed asynchronously.

```
$ (ls; date) & (who; ps)&
```

Example 4: Sequential Background Execution

In this example, only the **date** command is executed in the background after completion of the **ls** command:

```
$ ls; date&
```

In each of these examples, output from the commands is printed on the terminal. It is suggested (although not shown) that the output from the commands be redirected to a file.

Process Notes

Shell programs are executed through **fork** and **exec**, which create additional processes. Any commands invoked within the shell program are also executed via **fork** and **exec**. Therefore, when writing shell programs that invoke other shell programs, you must be careful that the maximum number of user and/or system processes is not exceeded. This is especially important when writing shell programs that may be used by more than one user at a time. Although the program by itself may not exceed the allowable number of user processes, multiple copies of it may exceed the maximum allowable number of system processes.

Where possible, use functions within shell programs. They do not create additional processes for execution.

Be considerate of other users when invoking background processes. The more processes simultaneously executing on a UNIX system, the slower the system as a whole will run. If possible, schedule large jobs to run in the background at night when processor load is lower (see the (**at(1)** and **nohup** commands).

BUILT-IN COMMANDS

These built-in commands are part of the shell. I/O redirection on these commands is allowed, with standard output being the default output file.

Return Values

If a built-in command executes correctly, it returns an exit code of 0. The following conditions will cause a non-zero exit code for the built-in command:

- Invalid options
- Incorrect number of arguments
- An incorrect argument
- Invalid I/O redirection
- Invalid variable assignment

KSH only

- Invalid alias name
- An attempt to expand a parameter that has not been set while the **nounset** option is in effect

---

: [arg ...]

Description

The : is a null operator and has no effect. The *args* to : are expanded.

Return Value

A zero exit code is returned from :.

. *file* [*file* ...]

Description

Commands in the file specified after the **.** (dot) built-in command are read and interpreted by the current shell. A subshell is not invoked. The search path specified by the *PATH* variable is used to find the directory containing the file to be read in by the **.** command.

Return Value

A zero exit code is returned if the file was found and read.

alias [**-tx**] [*name* [=*value*] ...]

KSH only

Description

An alias allows commands to be renamed within the shell. If an alias has been defined, the command for that alias is substituted when the alias is used.

The options to the **alias** built-in command are:

-t   This option is used to set and display tracked aliases. A tracked alias has the full path name for the command. If the *PATH* variable is changed, the alias becomes undefined but remains tracked. Tracked aliases execute faster because the shell does not have to search for the command.

-x   This option to the **alias** command causes the alias to remain in effect for shell programs that are invoked directly by their name and do not invoke a separate **ksh** process. Exported aliases do not migrate across separate invocations of the **ksh**; they must be put into the **ksh** environment file specified by the *ENV* variable (see "Invocation").

The **alias** command with no arguments lists the current aliases in effect. The current aliases are displayed, one per line, in the form *name=command*. If the **-x** or **-t** options also are specified, only exported or tracked aliases, respectively, are displayed.

If the command:

```
$ alias whou
```

is given, the value of **whou** is displayed if it is set. Otherwise, the error message `whou alias not found` is printed. If the **-x** or **-t** options are specified with the name of a preset alias, the **alias** command sets those attributes (export and tracked) for the named alias. An **alias** is defined as follows:

```
$ alias whou="who -u"
```

Notice that double quotation marks are used to prevent the shell from interpolating the spaces to the command **who -u**.

The first character of an alias name may be any printable character; all other characters must be valid *identifiers* (a-z, A-Z, or 0-9). However, using a built-in shell metacharacter as the first character of an alias name may cause conflict with the shell's interpolation of the alias.

The command can be any valid shell program or UNIX command and may include built-in shell metacharacters. However, the first word of each command of replaced text will not be tested for additional aliases.

If an alias ends in a blank (space or tab), the word following the alias also is checked for alias substitution.

In the following example:

```
$ alias dir="ls "
$ alias opts="-CF"
$ dir opts
Src/      status*      unit01.n
unit02.nunit03.n      unit04.n
```

dir is aliased as an **ls** command and followed by a space; **opts** are aliased as -CF; thus, the command `dir opts` is interpolated as an `ls -CF` command.

An alias is expanded when the shell first reads a shell program, not when the program is executed. To take effect, an alias must be defined before it is used within the shell program.

Quoting of alias values is important. Using double quotation marks expands any metacharacters to be performed when the alias is defined. Metacharacters to be expanded when the alias is used should be enclosed in single quotation marks.

The following *exported* aliases are compiled into the shell but can be unset or redefined:

```
echo='print -'
false='let 0'
functions='typeset -f'
history='fc -l'
integer='typeset -i'
nohup='nohup '
pwd='print - $PWD'
r='fc -e -'
true=':'
type='whence -v'
hash='alias -t'
```

Return Value

alias returns a zero exit code if all names are valid aliases and valid attributes are specified. Otherwise, a non-zero exit code (the value of the number of names that are not aliases) is returned.

bg [*%job*]

KSH only

Description

On systems that support built-in job control, the **bg** command puts the current job in the background. If *%job* is specified, that job will be put in the background.

break [*n*]

Description

break is used to exit from a `for`, `while`, or `until` loop. An argument *n* can be specified to indicate the number of levels to break.

cd [*dir*]

Description

By default, **cd** changes the current directory to the directory specified by the *HOME* variable. Otherwise, *dir* becomes the current working directory.

The shell variable *CDPATH* can be used to set a search path for the directory containing *dir*. *CDPATH* contains a list of directories to search, separated by colons (:).

The default path is the current directory, in which case **cd** attempts to change to *dir*. The current directory can be specified by a null path name that can appear immediately after the equal sign or between the colon delimiters anywhere in the path list.

For example, to set the current directory as the first directory of the search path list, use the following:

```
CDPATH=:$HOME:$HOME/bin:/usr/games
```

Each directory in the search path is searched for *dir*, unless *dir* begins with a slash. /*dir* is an absolute path name; the search path specified by *CDPATH* is not used.

The **cd** command cannot be used with the restricted shell **rsh**.

cd *old new*

KSH only

Description

In the **ksh**, the form:

```
cd old new
```

substitutes the string *new* for the string *old* in the current directory name *PWD* and then attempts to change to that directory.

Return Value

Returns a zero exit code if the **cd** command can change to the *dir* specified. Otherwise, returns a non-zero exit code.

continue [*n*]

Description

continue causes immediate return to the top of a `for`, `while`, or `until` loop. If an argument *n* is specified, **continue** resumes at loop number *n*.

echo [*args*]

Description

echo prints its *args* separated by blanks and a newline on the standard output. **echo** uses the following C-language-type escape conventions to represent built-in characters:

Convention	*Meaning*
\b	Backspace
\c	Do not print a newline at end of **echo** command
\f	Form feed
\n	Output a newline
\r	Carriage return (without newline)
\t	Tab
\v	Vertical tab
\\	Backslash. Beware of conflicts in the shell's use of the backslash (\). It should be quoted (with single or double quotation marks) or preceded by a backslash to prevent the shell from interpolating it.
\0*n*	*n* is a one-, two-, or three-digit octal code for an ASCII character. The digit 0 must always precede the *n*.

echo is often used within shell programs to produce prompts or diagnostic messages.

Return Value

Returns a zero exit code if successful; otherwise, returns a non-zero exit code.

eval [*command-line ...*]

Description

eval reads and executes a normal command line. Use **eval** when "hidden" variable substitutions may cause conflicts. **eval** has the same effect as forcing the shell to scan the command line twice before executing the command. In the following example:

```
$ DIR='$HOME'
$ echo $DIR
$HOME
$ eval echo $DIR
/usr/billh
$
```

the variable *DIR* was set to **$HOME** because $HOME
was enclosed in single quotation marks (which
prevented interpolation of the variable lead-in character
$). The **eval** executed the **echo** command after its
arguments had been expanded by the shell.

Return Value

Returns the exit code of the command executed by **eval**.

exec [*command-line ...*]

Description

exec executes the command line directly, without
creating a new process. In effect, the current shell is
overlaid with the command specified on the command
line. This command then returns to the parent of the
process that was running before the **exec**. Unless the
execed program was a shell, the command may return to
init (the initialization process), thus logging out the user,
as in the following example:

```
$ exec ls
chapt00.n
chapt01.n
chapt02.n
AT&T System V Unix
Login:
```

exec may be used also to rename or create new file
descriptors. To change standard input from the keyboard
to a file, use the **exec** command in the following form:

```
$ exec < file
```

All commands that normally read from standard input
now read from *file*.

To change output redirection from the terminal to a file, use the following form:

```
$ exec > file
```

All output from a command will now go into *file* instead of being displayed on the terminal.

To reassign input/output back to the keyboard/terminal, use the **exec** command with the virtual file /dev/tty:

```
# Reassign standard input
$ exec < /dev/tty
# Reassign standard output
$ exec > /dev/tty
To open new file descriptors, use the
  exec command as follows:
# Open file descriptor 4 for input
$ exec <&4
# Open file descriptor 5 for output
$ exec >&5
```

Return Value

Because **exec** overlays the current process, no exit codes are returned.

exit [*n*]

Description

exit causes the shell to terminate with the exit status of *n* (*n* can be a positive integer between 0 and 255). If *n* is omitted, the exit status is that of the last command executed.

export [*name* ...]

Description

If no arguments are supplied to the **export** command, a list is printed of all variables currently exported in the current shell. If one or more arguments is provided, the shell assumes that they are the names of variables to be exported. They are marked for automatic export to the environment of subsequently executed commands.

Note that function names cannot be exported. If you use **export** within a function, a new local variable is not created.

KSH only

    export is the same as **typeset -x**.

Return Value

    export always returns a 0 exit status.

---

fc [-e *editor*] [-nlr] [*first*] [*last*]

KSH only

Description

    The **fix** command (**fc**) provides access to the history file and is used with the command-line editor. The **fc** options are:

Option	Description
-e *editor*	Edit and execute preceding command using *editor*. If *editor* is not specified, **fc** uses value of *FCEDIT* as the editor. Default editor is /bin/ed.
-n	Suppress command numbering when listing commands
-l	List last *HISTSIZE* number of commands (default 16)
-r	Reverse order of commands

When editing of commands is complete, **ksh** displays, reads, and executes them.

The values *first* and *last* let you specify the range of commands on which **fc** will operate. The *HISTSIZE* variable is used to set the size of the command list to be maintained (default 16). You can specify *first* and *last* as positive numbers that indicate the command(s) to be fixed, negative numbers that are subtracted from the current command number, or a string that is used to match the most recent invocation of that command. If *last* is not specified, its value is set to that of *first*. If *first* and *last* are not specified, *first* is set to 16 if the -l option was specified; if -l is not specified, *first* is set to 1. *last* is then set to 1 (that is, the preceding command).

Return Value

fc returns the value of the last command reexecuted or, if the -l option was specified, a zero. Otherwise, a non-zero exit status is returned for invalid arguments or syntax errors.

fc -e - [*old* =new] [*command*]

KSH only

Description

This command allows reexecution of a previously executed command. The command is displayed before it is executed.

The preset alias **r** can be used in place of **fc -e -**, with or without *old=new* and *command*.

If *old=new* is specified, the string *old* will be replaced with the string *new* when the command is executed.

command specifies which command is to be reexecuted. The value of *HISTSIZE* limits the number of commands that can be reexecuted. The *command* can be specified as any of the following:

- Nothing. Simply enter **r** or **fc -e -**. The preceding command will be reexecuted.

- A string or partial string. For example, **r ca** would reexecute the last command that started with the string *ca*.

- A positive number that indicates which command in the *HISTSIZE* list to reexecute.

- A negative number that is subtracted from the current command number; for example, **r -2** would reexecute the second to the last command previously executed.

Return Value
The value of the last executed command is returned.

fg [%*job*]

KSH only

Description
This command brings %*job* into the foreground on systems that support built-in job control mechanisms. If %*job* is not specified, the current job is brought into the foreground.

getopts *optstring name* [*arg*]

KSH only

Description
getopts checks the positional parameters or the optional string *arg* for legal options.

A + or – begins the *arg* value. An *arg* not beginning with either of these characters delimits the end of the option list. A – – can also be used to delimit the end of the option list.

optstring contains the options that are to be processed by **getopts**. If an option is followed by a semicolon, then that option is expected to have an argument with it. The argument may or may not be separated from the option by spaces or tabs.

Each time **getopts** is invoked, it places the next option letter in the variable name. For example, a + is prepended to name if the *arg* is preceded by a +.

The index to the next *arg* is contained in the variable *OPTIND*. *OPTIND* is initially set to a 1 when a shell program is invoked. **getopts** places the option argument in the *OPTARG* variable, as required.

An *optstring* preceded by a : changes how **getopt** reacts when an option not contained in *optstring* is encountered. If *optstring* does not contain a :, **getopts** displays an error message and sets *name* to ?. Otherwise, the option letter is put in *OPTARG* and sets *name* to ? for an unknown option, or sets *name* to : for a missing option argument.

Return Value

getopts returns true until it encounters the end of an option list.

hash [-r] [*commands*]

Description

The shell remembers each executed command's location in the search path. **hash** causes the shell to print a list of each command's search path, with the number of times the command was invoked (*hits*) and a measure of work required to locate a command in the search path (*cost*). In situations in which the stored location of a command needs to be recalculated, the *hits* information is followed by an asterisk (*). *Cost* is incremented when the calculation is completed.

If a *command* is supplied to **hash**, *hits* is reset to 0. The **-r** option causes the shell to forget all remembered locations.

Note that shell built-in commands and functions are not remembered and thus are not shown as part of the **hash** table.

KSH only

> **hash** is a predefined alias of **alias -t**.

Return Value

> **hash** always returns a 0 exit code.

---

jobs [-l]

KSH only

Description

> The **jobs** command lists the active jobs. With the **-l** option, the process id's are printed also.

---

kill [-l] [-*sig*] *process* ...

Description

> **kill** sends *sig* to the specified *process*, which can be either a process id or a job number.
>
> *sig* can be given as a signal number of the name of a signal as listed by **kill -l**. Without -*sig*, a TERM (terminate) signal is sent.

let *arg* ...

KSH only

Description

let evaluates arithmetic arguments as separate expressions. Because each *arg* is evaluated separately, it is important to quote expressions that contain spaces or tabs. Likewise, because many of the operators used within **let** statements (see following list) also have special meaning to **ksh**, they must be quoted. If only a single expression is to be evaluated, the form *((expr))* may be used in place of **let**. When *((expr))* is used, spaces, tabs, and other special characters do not have to be quoted; they are processed as if they were enclosed in double quotation marks.

All calculations are done as long integers and are not checked for overflow conditions. The following operators, which are listed in decreasing order of precedence, are used:

Operator	*Meaning*
–	Unary minus. Changes sign of value given.
!	Logical negation
* / %	Multiplication, division, and remainder operators, respectively
+ –	Addition and subtraction operators
<= >= < >	Less than or equal to, greater than or equal to, less than, and greater than operators
== !=	Equal to and not equal to operators
=	Assignment operator

Parameters to the **let** command must be predefined and have a value. Up to nine levels of recursion (grouping) are allowed.

Return Value

let returns zero if the value of the last expression evaluated was non-zero. Otherwise, a non-zero exit code is returned.

newgrp [*group* ...]

Description

The **newgrp** command changes the user's group identification. With no arguments, the group is changed back to the group specified in the user's /etc/passwd file entry.

If the **-** argument is specified, the environment is changed to what would be expected if the user actually logged in again as a member of the new group.

Before **newgrp** can change a user's group identifications, the user must be listed in the /etc/group file as member of the new group.

The **id(1)** command can be used to determine the group in which the user currently is working.

Return Value

newgrp always returns an exit code of 0 because it is run, in effect, as a command in the form **exec newgrp group**.

print [-Rnprsu[*n*]] [*arg* ...]

KSH only

Description

print has replaced the **echo** command in the **ksh**. **echo** is aliased to **print -**. All **echo** conventions apply to the **print** command unless the **-R** or **-r** options are specified.

The following options are used with the **print** command:

Option	*Meaning*
–	Process anything following the – as an argument, even if it begins with a –
–R	Do not use the **echo** conventions and process anything that follows (other than an **–n**) as an argument, even if it begins with a –
–n	Do not add a trailing newline to the output
–p	All arguments to the **print** command are redirected to a co-process started with | &
–r	Do not use the **echo** conventions
–s	Redirect *arguments* into history file
–u	Redirect output to file descriptor *n*. Without *n*, file descriptor 1 is used; otherwise, file descriptor must be 1, 2, or a file descriptor previously opened with **exec** command. **–u** option redirects standard output of **print** but does not cause file to be opened and closed or file descriptor to be duplicated each time.

pwd

Description

Prints current working directory.

KSH only

The **pwd** command is defined as **print - $PWD** in the **ksh**.

read [-prsu[*n*]] [*name*?*prompt*] [*var1* *var2* ...]

Description

read reads one line from standard input and assigns the first word to *var1*, the second word to *var2*, etc. If more words than *vars* are entered, all leftover words are assigned to the last variable.

If no *vars* are given, read simply reads and ignores the input.

KSH only

The default *var* is the variable *REPLY*. If the option *name*?*prompt* is used and this is an interactive shell, the value of *prompt* will be displayed on the standard error.

The following options may be specified to the read command in the ksh only:

Option	Meaning
-p	Read input line from a co-process. The ksh disconnects from the co-process when an end-of file or error condition occurs.
-r	Do not append a newline on input text
-s	Save input line as a command in history file
-u	Read from file descriptor *n*. The default is file descriptor 0 (standard input). If file descriptor is other than 0 or 2, file must be opened with exec command before it is read from using -u.

Return Value

read returns a zero exit code unless an end-of-file is encountered, in which case a non-zero exit code is returned.

readonly [*name* ...]

Description

With no arguments, **readonly** prints a list of variables marked by the shell as read-only.

If *vars* are specified, the shell marks the variables as read only. A *readonly* variable cannot be set or changed.

> **KSH only**
> **readonly** is the same as **typeset -r**.

Return Value

readonly always returns a zero exit status.

return [*n*]>

Description

return is used only within functions; it causes a function to exit with a value of *n*. If *n* is not specified, the return status is that of the last command executed.

set
[— aefhkntuvx [args]]

> **KSH only**
>
> # **set** [-aefhkmnostuvx]
> # [-o *option* ...] [*arg* ...]

Description

There are two ways of invoking the **set** command. Certain *args* are valid for each way of invoking the command.

The **set** command is used to do the following:

1. Print a list of current variables and their values

2. Set arguments to the current shell

3. Set positional parameters for the current shell

With no arguments, **set** prints a list of all variables and their values in effect in the current shell. Any defined functions are printed also.

The **set** command accepts the following arguments:

Argument	*Meaning*
-a	Mark variables that are modified or created for export
-e	Exit immediately if a command exits with a non-zero exit status

---

KSH only

-e	Execute the ERR trap and exit immediately if a command exits with a non-zero exit status. The **-e** option is not enabled while the profile files are being read.

-f	Disable file-name generation
-h	Locate and remember functions as they are defined (normally, functions are located and remembered when executed)
-k	Place in the environment for the command all keyword arguments, not just those that precede command name

Argument	_Meaning_

KSH only

-m	Run background jobs in a separate process group; upon completion, print a message indicating the exit status

-n	Read commands but do not execute them

KSH only

-p	Privileged or protected mode. See following description of **set** for additional information.
-s	Sort positional parameters (the default in the **ksh**)

-t	Exit after reading and executing one command
-u	Treat unset variables as an error when substituting
-v	Print shell input lines as they are read
-x	Print commands and their arguments as they are executed
-	Turn off **-x** and **-v** options and stop examining arguments
- -	Do not change any options (useful in setting $1 to -)

Using + rather than - causes these options to be turned off. The command:

```
$ set $-
```

prints the current arguments that are set.

Other arguments to **set** are considered to be positional parameters and are assigned, in order, to **$1**, **$2**, etc. in the current shell. These parameters can then be accessed by their individual position address or through $* and $@ (see "Positional Parameters").

KSH only

The **-o** argument to the **set** command allows additional options to be displayed, set, or unset. With no *options*, **set -o** lists all the following options and their current status.

One of the following options may be specified along with the **-o** option:

Option	*Meaning*
allexport	Same as **-a**
bgnice	Causes **ksh** to run all background jobs at a lower priority
errexit	Same as **-e**
emacs	Turns on **emacs** command line editor mode
gmacs	Turns on **gmacs** command line editor mode
ignoreeof	Ignores end-of-file. The shell no longer exits when a Ctrl-D (**^D**) is received; **exit** must be used explicitly to exit the shell.
keyword	Same as **-k**
markdirs	A / is appended to all directory names resulting from file-name generation
monitor	Same as **-m**
noclobber	Existing files will not be overwritten with the > redirection operator. The notation >l must be used to overwrite an existing file.
noexec	Same as **-n**
noglob	Same as **-f**
nolog	Function definitions are not stored in the history file
nounset	Same as **-u**

Option	*Meaning*
privileged	On **ksh** versions newer than 06/03/86, this option, when set, restores the effective user id and effective group id to their values when **ksh** was invoked. If this option is turned off, the effective user id is set to the real user id and the effective group id.
	The **privileged** option is set whenever the effective user id is not equal to the real user id or the effective group id is not equal to the real group id. When **privileged** is set, processing of the **$HOME/.profile** is disabled and the file **/etc/suid_profile** is used instead of the file specified by the *ENV* variable value.
protected	In the 06/03/86 version of the **ksh**, the **protected** option is automatically turned on whenever the effective and real user id's are not equal and/or whenever the effective and real group id's are not equal. When this option is set, processing of the user's **$HOME/.profile** is disabled, the *PATH* variable is reset to the default value, and the file **/etc/suid_profile** is used instead of the file specified in the *ENV* variable.
trackall	Same as **-h**
verbose	Same as **-v**
vi	Sets **vi** command-line editing mode
viraw	Processes each character as it is typed in **vi** command-line editing mode
xtrace	Same as **-x**

test [*expression*]

Description

test evaluates *expression* and returns an exit code indicating whether the expression was true (0) or false (non-zero). A non-zero exit code is set also if the **test** command has no arguments.

The **test** command can be used in one of the following forms:

```
test expression
```

```
[ expression ]
```

KSH only

```
[[ expression ]]
```

Description

The *expression* consists of the following primitives:

Primitive	Meaning
-r *file*	True if file exists and is readable
-w *file*	True if file exists and is writable
-x *file*	True if file exists and is executable
-f *file*	True if file exists and is not a directory
-d *file*	True if file exists and is a directory
-c *file*	True if file exists and is a character special file
-b *file*	True if file exists and is a block special file
-p *file*	True if file exists and is a named pipe (fifo)
-u *file*	True if file exists and its set-user-ID bit is set
-g *file*	True if file exists and its set-group-ID bit is set

-k *file*	True if file exists and its sticky bit is set
-s *file*	True if file exists and its size is greater than zero
-t [*fildes*]	True if open file whose file descriptor number is *fildes* (1 by default) is associated with a terminal device
-z *s1*	True if length of string *s1* is zero
-n *s1*	True if length of string *s1* is non-zero
s1 = *s2*	True if strings *s1* and *s2* are equal
s1 != *s2*	True if strings *s1* and *s2* are not equal
s1	True if *s1* is not the null string
n1 **-eq** *n2*	True if the integers *n1* and *n2* are algebraically equal. Any of the comparisons **-ne**, **-gt**, **-ge**, **-lt**, or **-le** may be used in place of **-eq**.

KSH only

-L *file*	True if *file* is a symbolic link
file1 **-nt** *file2*	True if *file1* is newer than *file2*
file1 **-ct** *file2*	True if *file1* is older than *file2*
file1	True if *file1* is linked to *file2*

These primatives may be combined with the following operators:

Operator	**Meaning**
!	Unary negation operator
-a	Binary *and* operator
-o (*expr*)	Binary *or* operator parenthesis used for grouping

-a has higher precedence than **-o**. Note that all the operators and options are separate arguments to *test*. Note also that parentheses are meaningful to the shell and must be escaped.

If you own a file but its owner permission bit is not set, the test of that file (-r, -w, or -x) will return a non-zero even though the file may have the *group* and/or *other* bits set for that test (-r, -w, or -x permission). The correct exit status will be returned if you are super-user.

The = and != operators have a higher precedence than (and cannot be used with) the -r through -n operators. The = and != must always have arguments.

If more than one argument follows the -r through -n operators, only the first argument is examined; the others are ignored unless the second argument is either -a or -o.

Return Value

test returns a zero exit status if the evaluation is successful; otherwise, returns a non-zero exit status.

times

Description

times prints the accumulated user and system times for processes run from the shell.

trap [*command*] [*signal*] ...

Description

trap sets up a *command* to be executed when the shell receives a *signal*. With no arguments, **trap** prints the traps currently in effect. If no *command* is specified, all traps for *signal* are reset. If *command* is null (:, ' ', or " "), this shell and all commands it invokes ignore the signal. If *signal* is 0, *command* is executed when it exits the shell.

trap commands are executed in order of signal number. If a signal that is ignored on entry to the current shell is trapped, the command is not executed.

The following signals often are used with the **trap** command (see **signal(2)** in the *UNIX Programmers Reference Manual*):

Signal	Meaning
0	Special signal for the shell. Executes *command* when shell exits.
1	Hangup. Sent when loss of **DTR** is detected.
2	Interrupt. Sent when user presses Break key.
3	Quit. Sent when user presses Del key.
15	Software termination. Set when a program exits.

KSH only

sig can be specified as a signal number or name. (Use **kill -l** to obtain a list of signal names.) Additionally, the pseudosignals ERR and EXIT are defined for **trap**.

The ERR signal is used to execute the *commands* whenever a command has a non-zero exit code. The EXIT signal operates the same as signal **0**.

---

type [*command*]

Description

type indicates how the shell interprets each *command*. **type** prints whether the command is a function, shell program, shell built-in, or standard UNIX command.

typeset -f[tux] [*name*]

KSH only

Description

This form of the **typeset** command (with the **-f** option) is used to display function names and values and to set and unset function attributes.

The following options are used with **-f**:

Option	*Meaning*
-t	Turns on **xtrace** option for function (see **set** command)
-x	Exports function definition so that it remains in effect across shell programs which are not a separate invocation of the **ksh**
-u	Specifies that function *name* refers to an as yet undefined function. *(Note: this option is available only in* **ksh** *versions newer than that of 06/03/86.)*

To display function names and their definitions, the **typeset** command with the **-f** option is used. To display only function names, the **+f** option is used.

Because function names are stored in the history file, **typeset** will not display function names if the history file does not exist or the **nolog** option was in effect when the function was read (see **set**).

Use **typeset** as follows:

- To display a single function, use the **typeset** *name* command with no options.

- To display all functions with a given attribute, specify the option with no function names.

- To display all functions, use **typeset -f**.

typeset [-FLRZefilprtux[*n*] [*name* [=*value*]] ...]

KSH only

Description

The **typeset** command is used to:

- Set and unset various attributes for variables and parameters

- Set and unset the value of variables and parameters

- Display variables and parameters and their attributes and values

With no options, the **typeset** command displays all variables/parameters in effect, as well as their type (export, readonly, etc.). Given a *name*, **typeset** displays the attribute for that variable/parameter.

If the + option is used, only the names of current variables and parameters are printed. If a - option is specified, the names and values of all current variables and parameters are printed.

The following options can be used to set (by typing a - before the option) or unset (by typing a + before the option) various attributes for variables and parameters:

Option	*Meaning*
-u	Make variable uppercase.
-l	Make variable lowercase.

-i   Mark variable as an integer. An optional *n* can be specified to indicate the base. The following code, for example:

```
$ typeset -i2 binary=5
$ print $binary
2#101
```

sets the variable *binary* to 5, using base 2 notation. When the variable value is printed, the base is printed first, followed by a #; then the value is printed in the base notation.

-L   Left justify the variable value. An optional *n* may be specified to indicate the field width.

-LZ   Left justify the variable; strip leading zeros. An optional *n* may be specified to indicate the field width.

-R   Right justify the variable value. An optional *n* may be specified to indicate the field width.

-RZ   Right justify the variable. An optional *n* may be specified to indicate the field width and fill it with leading zeros.

-Z   Fill the field with leading zeros. (This option is equivalent to **-RZ**. An optional *n* may be specified to indicate the field width.)

-r   Mark variable/parameter as **readonly**.

-x   Mark variable as **export**ed.

-H   Map a UNIX system path name to a host operating system path name specification. (This option has no effect on UNIX systems.)

-t   User-defined tag

If **typeset** is used within a function, a local variable of the *name* specified is created. When the function exits, the variable's value and attributes (if any) are restored.

Return Value

typeset returns a zero exit status if no errors are encountered; otherwise, returns a non-zero exit status.

ulimit [-cdfmpt] [*n*]

Description

ulimit imposes a file size limit of *n* blocks for files written by the shell and any processes it executes. Files of any size may be read.

Without *n*, the current limit is printed. Any user may lower his or her limit, but only the super-user may raise a limit.

unalias *name* ...

KSH only

Description

The **unalias** command is used to remove aliases.

Return Value

unalias returns a zero exit code if all *name(s)* are valid aliases. Otherwise, a non-zero exit code is returned.

umask [*mask*]

Description

umask sets the file permission mask. If *mask* is not specified, the current mask is printed.

umask specifies which bits to *take away* when a file/directory is created. *mask* is an octal number in the range 000 to 777. This *mask* is the same as that used with the **chmod** command (see **chmod(1)** in the *UNIX User's Reference Manual*). *mask* specifies what permissions the system should remove when a file or directory is created.

The following values of **umask** are useful:

umask *Value*	*File Permission*	*Directory Permission*
000	-rw-rw-rw-	drwxrwxrwx
002	-rw-rw-r—	drwxrwxr-x
007	-rw-rw———	drwxrwx—
022	-rw-r—r—	drwxr-x—
027	-rw-r———-	drwxr-x—
077	-rw———-	drwx———

unset [-f] *name ...*

Description

unset removes the variable or function *name* from the current shell.

The **-f** option is used to specify unsetting of a function.

The variables *PATH*, *PS1*, *PS2*, *MAILCHECK*, and *IFS* cannot be unset.

Return Value

unset always returns a zero exit status.

wait [*n*]

Description

wait waits for a specified process *n* to complete and then reports its termination status. If *n* is not specified, all currently active child processes are waited for until they exit and the return status is a 0.

Return Value

If *n* is specified, the return code is that of the process waited for. This is an effective way to obtain the return status of background processes.

whence [-v] *name* ...

KSH only

Description

whence prints how a command would be interpreted. The **-v** option prints a more verbose report.

In the **ksh**, the **type** command is aliased as **whence -v**.

SHELL PARAMETERS AND VARIABLES

Shell *parameters* are used to store values for the current shell or subshells to use later. A parameter may be one of the following types:

- a positional parameter
- a special parameter
- a named parameter (variable)

Positional parameters have a number as their name. *Special parameters* have one of the following characters as part of their name: `* @ # ? - $ !`. A *named parameter* uses an identifier as part of its name and is often referred to as a *variable*.

A parameter value is available only to the current shell unless it is **export**ed (see **export** under "Built-In Commands"), in which case its value can be accessed by subshells that the current shell creates.

The character `$` is used to reference the value of a parameter. For example, `$LOGNAME` is read as "the value of the parameter *LOGNAME*."

There are no data types in the Bourne shell; all values are stored as character strings. The shell determines the data type when the parameter is used. For arithmetic functions in the Bourne shell, the **expr(1)** command must be used. **expr** is explained in the AT&T *UNIX User's Reference Manual*.

KSH only

Parameters can be declared as integers using the `typeset -i` command. The **ksh** also provides a built-in command, **let**, for performing arithmetic operations. (For additional information, see "Arithmetic Operations").

Positional Parameters

Positional parameters are values passed when a shell or subshell is invoked. Positional parameters are set as arguments to a shell script or by the **set** built-in command, and their names are numbers such as 1, 2, and so on. The name of the current command (shell script) is referenced as $0. Any additional parameters passed to the shell script are referenced as $1, $2, and so on. Only nine positional parameters can be directly referenced as $1 through $9 in the Bourne shell. The special parameters $@ and $* contain all the positional parameters starting with $1. The shell interprets $@ to mean "$1 $2 $3 $4 . ." and $* to mean "$1" "$2" "$3", and so on (see "Quoting" in the "Shell Basics" section).

KSH only

Positional parameters greater than $9 can be referenced with the notation **${*n*}**. Thus, ${13} refers to positional parameter 13.

The **ksh** also supports one-dimensional arrays in the range of 0 through 511. A parameter can be subscripted using [ ]. The value of an array element is accessed with the notation **${*var*[*n*]}**. Referencing a parameter (without a subscript) that is part of an array is the same as referencing the first parameter of the array (*parameter[0]*).

Parameter arrays do not need to be declared before use. Any reference to a parameter array with a valid subscript is acceptable and the array element will be created when it is first assigned.

Special Parameters

Special parameters are set automatically whenever a shell is invoked. These parameters have special meaning to the shell and cannot be modified directly. The following are the special parameters:

Variable	*Description*
$@	Positional parameters as "$1 $2 $3 $4 ..."
$*	Positional parameters as "$1" "$2" "$3" "$4", etc.
$#	The number of positional parameters passed to the shell
$-	The flags passed to the shell on invocation or set by the **set** command (see **set** under "Special Commands")
$?	The exit code of the last synchronously executed command
$$	The process number of the current shell
$!	The process number of the last background command invoked by the current shell

---

KSH only

$_ (Underscore)   This special parameter holds:

- The last argument of the previous command

- The name of the matching *MAIL* file when checking for mail

- The value of the pathname of each program **ksh** invokes; this value is then passed in the environment

This argument is not set for commands that are asynchronous.

Named Parameters

A *named parameter* is called a shell variable and it must start with a letter or underscore and can be followed by zero or more alphanumeric or underscore characters. To set a variable, enter the name of the variable, followed immediately by an = sign, followed immediately by the value:

```
firstname=John
```

If the value of a variable contains blanks (spaces or tabs) then the value must be quoted:

```
myname="John Smith"
```

The value of a variable may be accessed by preceding the variable with a **$**:

```
$ echo $firstname
John
```

If the value contains blanks, then you should quote the variable to prevent the shell from interpreting the blanks:

```
$ echo "$myname"
John Smith
```

Braces must be used for variable names that are followed by a letter, digit, or underscore which is not part of the variable name itself:

```
$ filename=chapt
$ echo $filename0
$ echo ${filename}0
chapt0
```

Variables Set by the Shell

___
KSH only

The shell sets the following variables:

Variable	*Description*
ERRNO	On versions of **ksh** newer than 06/03/86, this variable contains the integer value of the most recently failed system call. *ERRNO* is primarily used for debugging shell scripts. *ERRNO* is set only for errors that occur in the current process environment. Setting *ERRNO* to zero will clear its value.

Variable	Description
LINENO	In versions of **ksh** newer than the 06/03/86 version, *LINENO* is set to the current line number of a script or function before each command is executed. Often used as the value for the debug prompt `PS4`.
OLDPWD	This variable holds the previous working directory set by **cd.**
OPTARG	In versions of **ksh** newer than 06/03/86, *OPTARG* is set to the value of the argument of an option to **getopts**. See **getopts** for additional information on *OPTARG*.
OPTIND	In versions of **ksh** newer than 06/03/86, **getopts** sets *OPTIND* to the index of the argument to be processed. *OPTIND* is initially set to 1 whenever **ksh**, a shell script, or a function is invoked. Subsequently assigning *OPTIND* a value of 1 will reinitialize **getopts** to process another argument list.
PPID	Process number of the shell's parent.
PWD	Current working directory set by **cd** command.
RANDOM	Each time this parameter is referenced, a random integer is generated. Initialize the sequence of random numbers by assigning a numeric value to *RANDOM*.
REPLY	This variable contains the value entered on the terminal when no arguments are supplied to the **select** or **read** built-in commands.
SECONDS	This variable contains an integer value that indicates the number of seconds which have elasped since **ksh** was invoked. If *SECONDS* is assigned a value, then the variable will contain that value plus the number of seconds which have elasped since the assignment.

Variables Used by the Shell

The shell uses the following variables. These variables
are often set by the system administrator in the */etc/
profile* file or by each user in his or her own *.profile* file.
If values are not assigned to these variables, the shell
either:

- Assigns an explict default value that can be printed

- Assigns an implicit default value that cannot be
  printed

- Does not assign a value; in this case, use of the null
  variable value may yield undesired results

Variable	*Description*
CDPATH	Search path for the **cd** command. The *CDPATH* takes precedence over the current directory when searching for a subdirectory. Thus, you should include the current directory in *CDPATH* by using the dot (.) notation. Example:

```
CDPATH=."$HOME:/usr/project
```

KSH only

COLUMNS	If this variable is set, the value is used to define the width of the edit window for the shell edit modes and for printing **select** lists.
EDITOR	If the value of this variable ends in **emacs**, **gmacs**, or **vi** and the *VISUAL* variable is not set, then the corresponding option (see the discussion of **set** in the "Built-In Commands" section) will be turned on.

Variable	_Description_
ENV	If this parameter is set, then parameter substitution is performed on the value to generate the pathname of the script that will be executed when the **shell** is invoked. (See "Invocation" in the "Shell Basics" section). This file is typically used for **alias** and **function** definitions.
FCEDIT	Default editor name for the **fc** command.
FPATH	In versions of **ksh** newer than 06/03/86, this variable may be set to contain a colon (:) separated list of directories that **ksh** searches for a function definition file. The format of _FPATH_ is the same as the _PATH_ variable. _FPATH_ is used with the **autoload** alias ```(alias autoload='typeset fu')```
HISTFILE	If this parameter is set when the shell is invoked, then the value is the pathname of the file that will be used to store the command history.
HISTSIZE	If this parameter is set when the shell is invoked, then the number of previously entered commands that the shell can access will be greater than or equal to this number. The default is 128.

HOME	Default argument (home directory) for the **cd** command. This variable is set by **login(1)**.
IFS	Internal field separators, normally space, tab, and newline.

KSH only	
	In versions of **ksh** newer than the 06/03/86 release, _IFS_ cannot be exported for security reasons.

Variable	*Description*
LINES	This variable contains the number of lines on a terminal and is used by **ksh** to print **select** lists (see the **select** built-in command). **select** lists are printed vertically until about two-thirds of the value of *LINES* lines are filled. The default value of *LINES* is 24.
MAIL	If this variable is set to the name of a mail file and the *MAILPATH* parameter is not set, the shell informs the user that mail has arrived in the specified file. This variable is set by **login(1)**.
MAILCHECK	This parameter specifies how often (in seconds) the shell will check for the arrival of mail in the files specified by *MAILPATH* or *MAIL* parameters. The default is 600 seconds (10 minutes). If this parameter is set to 0, the shell will check before each prompt.
MAILPATH	A colon (:) separated list of file names. If this parameter is set, the shell informs the user that mail has arrived in any of the specified files. Each file name can be followed by a % and a message that will be printed when the modification time changes. The default message is *you have mail*.

KSH only

MAILPATH	This variable contains a colon (:) separated list of pathnames of mail files to be checked for the arrival of new mail. Each pathname can be followed by a ? and a message to be displayed when new mail arrives. The default message is *You have mail in [mailfile]*.

PATH	Search path for commands. Users cannot change *PATH* if executing under **rsh**.

Variable	*Description*
PS1	Primary prompt string, by default "$".
PS2	Secondary prompt string, by default ">".

KSH only

PS3	Selection prompt string used within a **select** loop, by default "#? .
PS4	Debug prompt string. The value of *PS4* is expanded and printed on the standard error output whenever the shell is ready to display a command during execution trace mode. The *LINENO* variable can be used as the *PS4* prompt to display the line number of the script or function that corresponds to the line displayed by **ksh**. For example:

```
PS4='$LINENO '
``` |

SHACCT	If this parameter is set to the name of a file writable by the user, the shell will write accounting records in the file for each shell procedure executed. Accounting routines such as **acctcom**(1) and **acctcms**(1M) can be used to analyze the data collected.
SHELL	When the shell is invoked, it scans the environment variables for this name. If it is found and there is an **r** in the file name part of its value (such as in **rsh** or **rksh**), the shell becomes a restricted shell.
TERM	This variable contains the type of terminal you currently are using. Although not used directly by the shell, this variable is used by many programs on UNIX for screen control.

Variable	*Description*

KSH only

TMOUT	If this variable is set to a value greater than zero, the shell terminates when a command is not entered within the prescribed number of seconds. (Note that the shell can be compiled with a maximum bound for this value which cannot be exceeded.)
VISUAL	If the value of this parameter ends in **emacs**, **gmacs**, or **vi**, then the corresponding option will be turned on (see the discussion of **set** in the "Built-In Commands" section).

Parameter Expansion

The shell provides a mechanism for conditionally evaluating parameters and performing substitution according to the parameter being *set*, *not set*, *null*, or *non-null*.

A parameter can be *set* or *not set*. If the shell has the parameter name in its internal list, then the parameter is considered to be set. The following shows how a parameter is set:

```
tmpdir=
```

This will place the parameter **tmpdir** in the parameter list but it will not have a value.

A parameter can be *null* or have a value (*non-null*). In the previous example, **tmpdir** is null.

You can use the following conventions to perform conditional substitution on parameters, depending on whether they are set, not set, null, or non-null:

Convention	Description
${var}	The value of *var* is substituted if it is non-null. The braces are used when a *var* is followed by a letter, digit, or underscore that could be misinterpreted as part of the *var* name. If *var* is a digit then it is a positional parameter. If *var* is a * or @ then all positional parameters, starting with **$1**, are substituted and separated by spaces.

KSH only

> If a parameter is subscripted (part of an array) then the braces must be used:
>
> ```
> $ user[5]="Tom Jones"
> $ print "${user[5]}"
> Tom Jones
> ```
>
> If an array *var* with a subscript of * or @ is used, then the values of all elements of the array, separated by spaces, are substituted.

Convention	Description
${var:-word}	If *var* is set and non-null, use its value. Otherwise, substitute *word*. Note the keyword here is *substitute*. If *var* is not set or is null, then *word* will be used; there will be no effect on *var*.
${var:=word}	If *var* is not set or is null, set it to *word* ; the value of *var* is then substituted. After conditional substitution with this notation, *var* will be set to *word*. Note: You can't assign positional parameters this way.
${var:?word}	If *var* is set and is non-null, substitute its value; otherwise, print *word* and exit from the shell. If *word* is omitted, the message `parameter null or notset` is printed.

${*var*:+*word*}   If *var* is set and is non-null, substitute *word*; otherwise substitute nothing.

KSH only

${#*var*}   The length of the value of *var* is substituted if *var* is not an *. Otherwise, the number of positional *var*s is substituted.

${#*identifier*[*]}}   The number of elements in the array *identifier* is substituted.

${*var*#*pattern*}
${*var*##*pattern*}   If the shell *pattern* matches the beginning of the value of *var*, then the value of this substitution is the value of the *var* with the matched pattern deleted; otherwise the value of this *var* is substituted. In the first form the smallest matching pattern is deleted and in the latter form the largest matching pattern is deleted.

${*var*%*pattern*}
${*var*%%*pattern*}   If the shell *pattern* matches the end of the value of *var*, then the value of *var* with the matched pattern is deleted; otherwise the value of *var* is substituted. In the first form the smallest matching pattern is deleted and in the latter form the largest matching pattern is deleted.

In the preceding structures, *word* is not evaluated unless it is to be used as the substituted string. If the colon (:) is omitted from the preceding expressions, then the shell checks only whether *var* is set.

The following examples illustrate how the parameter *TERM* would be set using two different conditional constructs:

```
TERM=${TERM:-dumb}
${TERM:=dumb}
```

PROGRAMMING CONSTRUCTS

for

Usage

> **for** *variable* **in** *words*
> **do**
> > *commands*
>
> **done**
> **for** *variable*
> **do**
> > *commands*
>
> **done**

Description

for executes *commands* for the number of *words* by setting *variable* to *word(1)*, *word*, etc. If no *words* are given, **for** executes the *commands* once for each positional parameter set on the command line.

Example

This first example runs **spell** on all files that match the pattern *unit??.n*; it redirects output to the file name followed by a *_sp*:

```
for i in unit??.n
do
   spell $i > $i_sp
done
```

To collect all output in a single file, the following form of **for** could be used. Notice where output redirection takes place:

```
for i in unit??.n
do
   echo "$i:"
   spell $i
   echo "\n"
done > spell.out
```

Return Value

for returns the exit code of the last command executed.

while

Usage

> **while** *command*
> **do**
>   *commands*
> **done**

Description

while executes *command*; if its exit status is zero (true), the **do** *commands* are executed. Execution continues until the **while** *command* exits with a non-zero (false).

Examples

This first example monitors the logged on user. As soon as he or she logs off, a message to that effect is printed:

```
while who | grep tom > /dev/null
do
    sleep 10
done
echo "Tom just logged off"
```

The next example processes all the arguments to a shell script using $# (the number of positional parameters).

```
while [ $# -ne 0 ]
do
    spell $1 > $1.out
    shift
done
```

Return Value

The exit status of the last **do** *commands* command is returned unless no commands are executed, in which case the **while** *command* returns a zero.

until

Usage

until *command*
do
   commands
done

Description

until executes *command* and, if its exit status is non-zero (false), the **do** *commands* are executed. Execution continues until the **until** *command* exits with a zero (true).

Example

The following script monitors for a user logging on to the system:

```
until who | grep tom > /dev/null
do
    sleep 10
done
echo "Tom just logged on"
```

Return Value

The exit status of the last **do** *commands* command is returned unless no commands are executed, in which case the **until** *command* returns a zero.

if

Usage

> **if** *command*
> **then**
> > *commands*
>
> **fi**
> **if** *command*
> **then**
> > *commands*
>
> **else**
> > *commands*
>
> **fi**
> **if** *command*
> **then**
> > *commands*
>
> **elif** *command*
> **then**
> > *commands*
>
> **fi**

Description

The *command* following the **if** is executed; if it returns a zero (true) exit status, the *commands* following the **then** are executed. The keyword **fi** is used to terminate the **fi** statement.

If the **if** *command* returns a non-zero, the **else** *commands* are executed.

The **elif** *command* is executed if the **if** *command* returns a non-zero exit status. The **then** *commands* associated with the **elif** *command* are executed if the exit status is zero.

Examples

The following example illustrates how the **if** statement can be used to evaluate a command's output:

```
if who | grep tom > /dev/null
then
     echo "Tom is logged on"
fi
```

In the next example, **if** is used with the `else` statement to print the type of file:

```
if [ -f status ]
then
    echo "status is a regular file"
else
    echo "status is not a regular file"
fi
```

To provide additional information, the **elif** construct can be used:

```
if [ -f status ]
then
    echo "status is a regular file"
elif [ test -d status ]
then
    echo "status is a directory"
fi
```

Return Value

The **if** returns a zero exit status if no **else** *command* or **then** *commands* are executed; otherwise, the status of the last executed command is returned.

case

Usage

case *word*
in

    pattern1)
    commands
    ;;
    pattern2)
    commands
    ;;
esac

Description

The **case** command executes the *commands* associated with the first *pattern* that matches *word*. Each pattern must be terminated by a double semicolon (; ;). Patterns are the same as those used for file-name generation.

Example

The following example shows how users can be limited to execute only certain commands:

```
echo "Enter command: \c"
read cmd
case $cmd
in
    ls)
      /bin/ls ;;
    who)
      /bin/who ;;
    date)
      /bin/date ;;
      *)
       echo "Invalid command" ;;
esac
```

Notice the use of the asterisk (*) to match everything else (normally called the *default case*).

Return Value

case returns the exit status of the last command executed.

(command list)

Usage

(*command1*; *command2*; ...)
(*command1*& *command2*& ...)

Description

This construct is called *command grouping*. The **command list** is executed in a subshell. The output of the group is sent to standard output and can be piped to another command or redirected into a file.

If the commands are separated by semicolons, each command is executed in sequence. If the commands are separated by ampersands, each command is executed in the background.

Example

In the following command list, all three commands are executed as a group, with output going to a file named *status*:

```
(date;ls;who) > status
```

Return Value

The exit status of the last command in the list is returned.

{ command list }

Usage

```
{ command1; command2; ...; }
{ command1& command2& ...& ;}
```

Description

The command list is executed in the current shell. The output of the group is sent to standard output. Any environmental changes made by the commands in the list are effected in the current shell.

A space must follow the left brace ({); a semicolon (;) must follow the last command.

Example

In the following example, all three commands are executed by the current shell; output is sent to a file named *status*:

```
{ date;who;ls; } > status
```

Return Value

The exit status of the last command in the list is returned.

functions

Usage

name( )
{
    commands
}
function
{
    commands
}

Description

A function of **name** is defined. The function identifier must be followed by left and right parentheses.

KSH only

The keyword **function** is used to define a function of *name*.

Functions are read into the current shell process and stored internally in the current shell process. To call a function, simply enter it as the name of a command (note that function names should never be the same as those of existing UNIX commands or built-in shell commands). Commands within braces are executed when the function is called.

A function has access to the variables set for the current shell.

KSH only

The **typeset** special command used within a function defines a variable as local to the function. The variable's scope is local to the current function and any functions it calls. The calling process will not have access to the variable, since the variable is unset when the function exits.

The **typeset -f** command can be used to list functions and their text; the **unset -f** command, to undefine functions.

Example

This example shows how the **ls** command can be redefined to list the files in columns:

```
ls()
{
    /bin/ls -C
}
```

Notice the use of the full path name when naming functions with the same name as an existing command. (This scheme will not work for built-in shell commands.)

Return Value

The exit status of the last command in a function is returned unless an explicit return value is set with the **return** built-in special command (see "Built-In Commands").

select

Usage

```
select variable in words
do
      commands
done
select variable
do
      commands
done
```

Description

The **select** command prints the *words* on the standard error output, each preceded by a number. If *words* are omitted, as in the second example of usage, the positional parameters are used.

Then the **PS3** prompt is printed and a line is read from the standard input. If the line matches the number of one of the listed *words*, the value of *variable* is set to the *word* matching the corresponding number selected. If the line is empty, the selection list is printed again. If the line does not match one of the selection numbers, the *variable* is set to null.

The line read from the standard input is saved in the *REPLY* variable. The *commands* are executed for each *selection* until a BREAK or end-of-file is encountered.

Example

The following example illustrates a simple menu using the **select** command:

```
PS3="Enter item: "
select choice in ls date who quit
do
    case $REPLY
    in
      1)
          ls ;;
      2)
          date ;;
      3)
          who ;;
    4|Q|q)
          exit ;;
      *)
          print "Invalid Choice" ;;
    esac
done
```

time

Usage

time *command*

Description

Command is executed and the amount of real, user, and system time it took to execute is printed. **time** is useful for checking the efficiency of shell programs. For example:

```
$ time status
real    0m1.61s
user    0m0.16s
sys     0m1.31s
```

SHELL PROGRAMS

A shell program is simply a file that contains built-in shell commands, functions, and UNIX commands. Shell programs frequently are used when a sequence of commands must be executed more than once.

Creating and Executing Shell Programs

To create a shell program you use your favorite editor to enter the commands into a file.

To execute a shell program, you can do either of the following:

- Change the mode of the file so that it is executable, and then enter its name on a command line as you would enter other UNIX commands

- Invoke it, using the **sh** command with options, as in the following examples:

  ```
  $ sh myprog
  ```

  or

  ```
  $ sh -x myprog
  ```

In both of these methods of execution, a subshell is created to execute the commands within the file.

The name of a shell program should not be the same as that of an existing UNIX command, a built-in shell command, or a function. Remember that the shell first executes built-in commands, then functions, then UNIX commands or shell programs. A common mistake is to name a shell program *test*, only to discover that the shell program does not execute because **test** is a built-in shell command, which is executed before the shell program. The same holds true for all other built-in shell commands.

Giving a shell program the same name as an existing UNIX command has the following undesired effects:

- The shell program is executed in place of the UNIX command (if the *PATH* variable is set to search local directories first)

- The UNIX command executes instead of the shell program (if the *PATH* is set to search first for system commands)

Debugging Shell Programs

If the shell encounters an error while executing a shell program, it terminates execution and returns a non-zero exit status. Several methods may be used to help find the error.

First, the shell program should be closely examined to determine whether the program is syntactically correct (all quotes in balance, correct spelling of commands, etc.).

Next, the **-x** option can be used as follows:

```
$ sh -x myprog
```

to print the commands and their arguments as they are executed. The **-x** option can be turned on also by placing the line `set -x` anywhere in the shell program file itself. This option lets you watch the execution of the shell program and determine where it is failing.

In another method of debugging, **echo** commands are placed in the file to print out information as the shell program is executed. **echo** commands can be used to print the value of variables or, if **echo** precedes a command, will print out how the command would be interpreted by the shell:

```
echo "rm chapt??.n"
rm chapt01.n chapt02.n chapt03.n
```

For a "divide and conquer" method of debugging, use the **exit** command. By having the program exit at various places, you can test specific portions of the program to determine exactly where the problem lies.

Using the Dot Command

When a shell program is invoked either by its name or by running the shell with the name of a program as its argument (as in **sh prog1**), a separate subprocess is created to execute commands within the program. Changes made to the environment from within the program, such as changing directories, creating new variables, or changing the values of variables, do not remain when the program exits.

The dot (.) command causes the current process to execute the program directly, in its environment. Arguments can be passed to a program invoked with the . command.

The dot command is commonly used, for example, when changes are made to a user's .profile file. Instead of logging out and then logging back on to have the changes take effect, the user simply enters the following command:

```
$ . .profile
```

to force the login shell to read and execute the commands within the .profile file.

Used from within shell programs, the . command is very useful for reading files that contain variable assignments and function declarations. Instead of entering variable assignments and functions into each shell program, use the . command to read the file that contains them.

Shell Program Examples

Processing Command-line Arguments

A shell program commonly is used to process command-line arguments and generate a new command line before invoking a UNIX command. The following examples illustrate various methods of processing command-line arguments.

```
# Checking number of
# command-line arguments
if [ $# -ne 5 ]  # Arguments not equal
                 # to 5
then
    echo "Usage: $0 args"
fi


# Using a for loop
# to process arguments
for arg # Default word list
do
    echo $arg
done


for arg in $* # Wordlist is all
              # arguments
do
    echo $arg
done


# Using a while loop
# to process arguments
while [ $# -ne 0 ] # Check number of
                   # arguments
do
    echo $1 # Process first argument
    shift   # Shift $2 to $1, etc.
done


while [ "$1" ] # Check $1
               # not the null string
do
    echo $1 # Process $1
    shift   # Shift $2 to $1, etc.
done


# This example allows the user to
# specify a command-line
# argument. If no argument is
# supplied, the program prompts
# for one.
```

```
if [ $# -eq 0 ]
then
     echo "File Name: \c"; read fname
else
     fname=$1
fi
```

Data Management

The shell can be used as a data-management tool with ASCII files that have a *record-field structure*. A good example of this type of file is /etc/passwd. Each line represents a *record* for a user on the system; within each line, a colon separates the *fields*.

The following program shows how the shell can be used to read each line and separate the fields:

```
IFS=: # Set the input field separator
to :
exec < /etc/passwd # Redirect stdin
from /etc/passwd
while read line # Read a line from
stdin (/etc/passwd)
do
     set — $line # Set positional
parameters
     echo "Login: $1"
     if [ ! "$2" ]
     then
     echo "Passwd: None"
     else
        echo "Passwd: Set"
     fi
done
```

In this sample program, **exec** is used to redefine where the input is taken from. Then the while loop continues to read a line from /etc/passwd until end-of-file is reached. Each time a line is read, **set** uses the value of *IFS* (:) to set the positional parameter.

Programming Hints

The following hints can help make your programs run faster and more efficiently:

1. Use shell built-in commands wherever possible. Unlike UNIX commands, they do not cause creation of subprocesses.

2. Take advantage of a command's capabilities. For example, because **sort** can open files,

   ```
   sort file
   ```

   is much more efficient than

   ```
   cat file | sort
   ```

3. Use input and output redirection. For example:

   ```
   $ lp < file
   ```

   is better than

   ```
   $ cat file | lp
   ```

4. Use **exec** to invoke subshells that do not need to return to the parent; or, to return to the parent, use **exec** in both the parent and in the child.

5. Think about the number of bytes to be processed.

   ```
   $ grep pattern file | sort
   ```

   requires the **sort** command to process less bytes than

   ```
   $ sort file | grep pattern
   ```

6. Use functions within your shell programs. They execute much faster than subshells.

7. Use the dot (.) command to invoke subshells that modify variables. If you use the dot command, you won't have to pass information back and forth between the two programs.

8. Use command substitution instead of the pipeline mechanism. For example, use

```
$ sort `cat file`
```

instead of

```
$ cat file | sort
```

because more overhead is needed for creating the pipe mechanism than for using command substitution.

9. Redirect the output of commands within a loop once, at the end of the loop, instead of after each command. For example, use the following:

```
for i in 01 02 03 04 05
do
   sort unit$i
done > tmp
```

instead of

```
for i in 01 02 03 04 05
do
   sort unit$i >> tmp
done
```

The output of loops can also be piped to a command:

```
for i in 01 02 03 04
do
   sort unit${i}
done|lp
```

instead of

```
for i in 01 02 03 04
do
   sort unit${i} | lp
done
```

10. Use pipes instead of creating temporary files, wherever possible:

```
cat unit?? | tr [a-z] [A-Z]
```

instead of

```
cat unit?? > tmp
tr [a-z] [A-Z] < tmp
```

11. Become familiar with all the UNIX commands so that you can choose the most efficient one to do the job. For example, **find** is more efficient than **ls** in some cases:

```
$ find . -type d -print
```

is faster than

```
# Find directories
$ ls -lR | grep "^d"
```

Similarly, sometimes **awk** is better to use for searching and processing information in a file than **grep** or **sed**.

12. Plan file-naming and directory structures before you begin a project. Using shell metacharacters (wild cards) is more efficient than using shell programs that build lists of file/directory names.

13. The shell uses the *PATH* variable to locate commands. To improve performance, set up your search path (in the *PATH* variable) or organize your directory structure so that the shell doesn't have to make extensive searches.

14. Use the **cd** command in shell scripts to change to a directory before processing files or executing commands. The shell can locate files and commands and file more quickly if they are in the local directory. In the following shell script:

```
for i in /usr/john/documents/
    book1/*
do
    format $i
done
```

each name in the list will contain */usr/john/ documents/book1*. Parsing will take longer and you could overflow the "wordlist" buffer.

A better method, using **cd**, follows:

```
cd /usr/john/documents/book1
for i in *
do
format $i
done
```

15. Keep files and directories small, when possible. File access is much faster on small (<10K) files; directory searches are much faster on small directories (<286 entries).

16. Have your programs clean up temporary files upon exit.

RELATED UNIX COMMANDS

The following commands are not part of the shell but are extremely helpful when you write shell programs. (For a complete description of these commands, see the *AT&T UNIX User's Reference Manual*.)

basename *pathname* [suffix]

Description

basename prints the last part of a *pathname*. If *suffix* is given as an option to **basename**, then it too will be removed from *pathname* if present. **basename** is normally used within command substitution marks in shell programs. For example, the following will print only the name of a shell script, regardless of whether a full or partial pathname was supplied:

```
echo 'basename $0'
```

The following example can be used to strip off the trailing **.c** suffix from C program source code files:

```
for i in *.c
do
    basename $i .c
done
```

Return Value

basename always returns a zero exit status.

cat [*file(s)*]

Description

cat concatenates and prints *file(s)* on the standard output. If no *file(s)* are given or a - is given as an argument, **cat** will read from the standard input.

Use caution when redirecting the standard output to a file. The shell sets up I/O redirection before the **cat** command is invoked. Therefore, the command

```
$ cat unit01.n unit02.n > unit01.n
```

will not work as expected. You would end up with a 0 length *unit01.n* file. The command

```
$ cat unit01.n unit02.n > unit01.new
```

would produce the desired results.

Return Value

A zero exit status is returned if **cat** can successfully print the file. Otherwise, a non-zero exit status is returned.

chmod *mode file/directory*

Description

chmod changes the file access permissions according to the *mode* on the *file* or *directory* specified. Only the owner of the file or directory, or the superuser, may change permissions.

mode may be specified as an *octal* value or *symbolic* value. The format of the octal method is.

```
chmod mode file/directory
```

An octal value is determined by combinations of the following:

**Permission**	_**Octal Value**_
Owner	
Read	4
Write	2
Execute	1
Group	
Read	4
Write	2
Execute	1
Other	
Read	4
Write	2
Execute	1

For example, to change the mode of a file so only the owner and group members can read and write it, you enter the following command:

```
$ chmod 666 file
```

The format of the symbolic method is:

```
chmod who op permission file/directory
```

The following symbols are used to determine `who`, `op`, and `permission`:

who		**operator**		**permission**	
user	**u**	add	**+**	read	**r**
group	**g**	take away	**–**	write	**w**
other	**o**	absolute	**=**	execute	**x**
				suid/sgid	**s**

The following example shows how the write and execute permissions would be taken away for group and other access:

```
$ chmod og-wx file
```

Using the symbolic method, you can also specify more than one `op` by separating them with a comma (,):

```
# Add write permission for user, take
# away write and execute for group, and
# take away all permissions for others.
$ chmod u+w,g-wx,o-rwx file
```

Notice that there are no spaces between the `op` symbols in the above example.

Return Value

If it can change the mode, **chmod** returns a zero exit status. If the user is not the owner of the file/directory or the superuser, **chmod** fails and returns a non-zero exit status.

cp *file(s) target*

Description

cp copies the file(s) specified to *target*. *target* can be a directory, existing file, or new file. Multiple file names can only be specified when *target* is a directory.

If *target* is a directory, then all files will be copied into that directory with the same file names. If *target* is an existing file, then the original file is copied to it and the mode, owner, group, and links remain intact. If *target* is a new file, then the original file is copied to it and the mode, owner, and group of the new file remain the same as the old file.

Return Value

If the copy is successful, **cp** returns a zero exit status. Otherwise, a non-zero exit status is returned.

date [+*format*]

Description

The **date** command prints the current date and time on the standard output in the form of

```
Sat May 19 12:38:57 EDT 1990
```

date uses the value of the *TZ* variable to convert the system time to local time (UNIX stores the time as Greenwich Mean Time).

An optional format string, preceded by a % sign, can be specified to print the date in a format more useful for your shell program. The format strings and their meanings are the following:

Format String	*Meaning*
n	Insert a newline character
t	Insert a tab character
m	Print the month of year (01 to 12)
d	Print the day of month (01 to 31)
y	Print the last 2 digits of year (00 to 99)
D	Print the date in MM/DD/YY format
H	Print the hour (00 to 23)
M	Print the minute (00 to 59)
S	Print the second (00 to 59)
T	Print the time in HH:MM:SS format
j	Print the day of the year (001 to 366)
w	Print the day of the week (Sunday = 0)
a	Print the abbreviated weekday (Sun to Sat)
h	Print the abbreviated month (Jan to Dec)
r	Print the time in AM/PM notation

Using the **date** command with one of these format strings is very useful within shell programs. For example, to set a variable equal to the current date as MM/DD/YY, use the following:

```
today=`date +%D`
```

Return Value

If the conversion is successful, **date** returns a zero exit status. A non-zero exit status is returned if the conversion fails or an invalid format specification character is entered.

dirname *pathname*

Description

dirname prints the initial part of *pathname*. For example, to find out the file system a user is on, use

```
$ echo $HOME
/usr/tom
$ filesys=`dirname $HOME`
$ echo $filesys
/usr
```

Return Value

dirname always returns a zero exit status.

env [-] [*name = value*] [*command*]

Description

The **env** command obtains the current environment, modifies it according to its arguments, and then executes a command with the modified environment. The - flag causes the inherited environment to be completely ignored so that the command is executed with only the environment specified by *name=value* pairs.

Like the **set** command, **env** will print the current environment if no arguments are specified.

env is a stand-alone UNIX command and is not part of the shell. **env** is useful for modifying the current shell environment prior to a command execution.

Return Value

env returns a zero exit status if its arguments and commands are successful; otherwise, the exit status will be that of the command.

expr *expression*

Description

expr is an expression evaluator used for evaluating strings and performing mathematical functions. **expr** is used in the Bourne shell for performing arithmetic operations, and is used in either shell when the **test** command does not provide the particular operation you need.

For example, to increment the value of a variable, use

```
# Increment i by 1
i=`expr $i + 1`
```

Return Value

expr returns a zero exit status if the evaluation is successful; otherwise, a non-zero exit status is returned.

false

Description

false always returns a non-zero (255) exit status. It can be used to control an **until** loop as follows:

```
until false
do
   ...
done
```

Return Value

false always returns a non-zero exit status.

find *directory expr*

Description

find is used to locate files and directories that match the values specified in *expr*. The first argument to **find** must be a starting *directory*. The following expressions can be used to construct the *expr* for files and directories to locate:

Expression	_Meaning_
-print	Always true. Prints the current pathname.
-name *filename*	Specifies the name of a file/directory to find. Returns true if the file/directory is found.
-perm *mode*	True if *mode* exactly matches the mode of a file/directory. If *mode* is prefixed by a - -, more flag bits are compared.
-type *t*	True if the type of file is *t*. *t* can be **d** for a directory or **f** for a file.
-size [+/-] *n*	True if the size of the file is *n* blocks long. If *n* is followed by a *c*, then the comparision is made for characters.
-mtime [+/-] *n*	True if the file was modified in the last *n* days. **-atime** can be used for access time and **-ctime** can be used for file creation time.
-exec *command*	*command* is executed on the found files. True if the command was successful. The end of the command must be punctuated with an escaped semicolon (\ ;).

A + in front of a number indicates greater than, and a - means less than. The following operators can be used to combine *expr*essions:

Operator	*Meaning*
!	Unary negation operator
-a	Binary and operator
-o	Binary or operator

The following are examples of uses for the **find** command:

```
# Find all files in the current
# directory that are readable by others
$ find . -type f -perm -002 -print
# Change the mode on all files
# so they are not writable by
# group and others
$ find . -type f -exec chmod og-w {} \;
```

find returns a zero exit status if the expression evaluates true. Otherwise, a non-zero exit status is returned.

grep [*opts*] *pattern* [*file(s)*]

Description

grep searches each of the file(s) specified for *pattern* and, without any options, prints each matching line on the standard output. If more than one file name is given on the command line, then the name of the file will also be printed preceding each matching line.

grep uses patterns in the form of regular expressions. The following table describes a number of useful options to **grep**:

Option	*Meaning*
-i	Ignore upper/lowercase distinction when making comparisons
-l	Only display the name of the file (once) for each file with a matching pattern
-c	Print a count of matching lines

The following examples may be useful with shell scripts:

```
# Find all files that contain UNIX
$ grep UNIX *
# Build a list of files that contain FL
flist=`grep FL *`
# Count the number of records in a file
# which have the pattern "Manager"
grep -c Manager employees
```

If the *pattern* consists of more than one word or contains special characters that are meaningful to the shell, then the pattern must be enclosed in quotes (" or ").

Be careful of the following:

```
# Find a greater-than (>) symbol in
# a file
$ grep > employees
```

In this example, the terminal appears to hang until the Del or Break key is pressed. You will then find that the file *employees* has been truncated to 0 length. This is because the **grep** command looked for something (a special character, >) from the standard input and when **grep** found the greater than symbol, the shell sent the output to the file *employees*. Because *employees* already existed, it was truncated to 0 before **grep** was invoked. The correct command syntax is

```
$ grep ">" employees
```

Return Value

grep returns a non-zero exit status if the pattern was found. An exit status of 1 is returned if no patterns were found in the file(s). An exit status of 2 is returned for syntax errors.

id

Description

id is used to print the real user and group id numbers and names. **id** prints a line on the standard output as follows:

```
uid=100(bill) gid=1(other)
```

If the effective and real user or group ids are different then both are printed:

```
uid=100(bill) gid=1(other)
   euid=102(tom) egid=3(sys)
```

Return Value

id always returns a zero exit status.

kill [-*sig*] PID

Description

The **kill** command is used to terminate a process. Without *sig*, **kill** sends a signal 15 (terminate) to the process specified by PID. A **kill -15** normally kills processes that do not catch or ignore signals.

If a number is specified as -*sig*, then the corresponding signal is sent to the process. A **kill -9 PID** will terminate any process.

Only the owner of a process or the superuser can kill a process.

Return Value

kill returns a zero exit status if it was able to terminate the process; otherwise, a non-zero exit status is returned.

ln *file(s) target*

Description

ln links *file(s)* to *target*. If *target* is a directory, then the files are linked into that directory with the same name as the original file. If *target* is a file, then the original file is linked to the new file name. The new file must not exist before the **ln** command is invoked.

ln is useful for creating multiple references to a single file. It is especially useful when the original file is large. However, the permissions on linked files should be set so that the files are only readable by a group and others, to prevent multiple updates from being made at the same time.

Files cannot be linked across file systems.

Return Value

If the link is successful, **ln** returns a zero exit status. Otherwise, a non-zero exit status is returned.

lp [*file(s)*]

Description

lp directs the named files to the line printer spooler. An optional **-d** *dest* may be specified to route the print job to another printer other than the system default printer.

lp uses the shell variable *LPDEST* if it is set to determine the default printer destination for the user.

ls [*opts*] [*file/directory*]

Description

The **ls** command is used to list files and directories. Without any options or without a file/directory name specified, **ls** will list all of the files in the current directory. If the name of a file is specified, only that file is listed. If a directory name is given, then the files/directories in the specified directory are listed.

There are many options to the **ls** command. Some of the more commonly used options are the following:

Option	*Meaning*
-l	Produce a long listing showing file access permissions, link count, owner, group, size, the date that the file was last modified, and the name of the file.
-a	List all files and directories, even those beginning with a . (dot).
-t	List the files in sorted order according to the time they were last modified, with the most recent file being listed first.
-r	List the files in reverse order.
-C	List the files in columns.
-F	Display a trailing / after directory names and an * after executable files.

Return Value

A zero exit status is returned if the **ls** is successful. Otherwise, a non-zero exit status is returned and a diagnostic message is printed.

mkdir *directory*

Description

mkdir creates a new directory named *directory*. The mode of the new directory is set to 777 minus the permissions specified by **umask**.

mkdir requires that the parent directory have write permission set for the user making the new directory.

Return Value

If the new directory was created successfully, **mkdir** returns a zero exit status. Otherwise, a non-zero exit status is returned and **mkdir** displays an error message.

mv *file(s) target*

Description

mv moves or renames the specifed files to *target*. The *file* and *target* cannot be the same.

If *target* is a directory, then the named file(s) are moved into the directory with their same names. If *target* is the name of an existing file, mv first determines whether the file can be overwritten. If so, then the file is moved to the *target* file name. If the *target* file cannot be written to, then mv prints the *target* file permission mode and asks for a response. mv then reads from the standard input for a line beginning with a y and moves the file if permissible. Otherwise, mv exits with a non-zero exit status.

mv requires write permission for the directory that the file is to be moved into. mv does not require write permission on the file.

The -f option to mv can be specified to suppress the prompting for the move on existing files that do not have write permission.

Return Value

If the move is successful, mv returns a zero exit status. Otherwise, a non-zero exit status is returned.

nohup *command*

Description

nohup runs *command* with HANGUP and QUIT signals ignored. If output is not redirected then both standard output and standard error are sent to a file named *nohup.out*.

nohup is useful to start commands in the background and then log off. For example, a large sort job may be started at the end of the day.

Return Value

If the command can be executed, **nohup** returns a zero exit status. Otherwise, a non-zero exit status is returned.

pg *opts file(s)*

Description

pg displays the named files on the terminal a screenful at a time. After each screenful of information, **pg** pauses and displays a colon (:) prompt. The following commands can be entered at the prompt:

Command	Meaning
Space bar	Display the next screenful of information
Minus sign (–)	Display the previous screenful of information
h	Display help information
q	Quit

In addition to the preceding commands, **pg** accepts regular expressions as search patterns and skips to the appropriate position in the file that matches the regular expression.

Return Value

If **pg** can open and paginate the file(s), a zero exit status is returned. A non-zero exit status is returned for non-existent files, invalid arguments, or syntax errors.

rm [*opts*] *file(s)*

Description

rm removes specified files. Removal of a file requires write permission for the directory the file is in but does not require write or read permission for the file itself.

If the file does not have write permissions for the user attempting to remove it, then the **rm** command displays the file's permissions and prompts for input from the terminal. Entering a y causes the file to be removed if the user can write in the file's directory. Entering anything other than a y will not remove the file.

The following options are used with the **rm** command:

Option	*Meaning*
-f	Forcibly remove the file if possible. This option suppresses the prompting for removal of files that do not have write permission and suppresses error messages for non-existent files.
-r	Recursively remove files and directories. **rm** first removes all files in a directory and then removes the directory itself.
-i	Interactively remove files, asking the users whether they want to delete each file. A y entry causes the file to be deleted. Any other entry does not remove the file.

Return Value

A zero exit status is returned if the file was successfully removed or the **-f** option was specified. A non-zero exit status is returned if the user does not have permission to remove the file.

rmdir *directory*

Description

rmdir removes the *directories* specified as arguments to it. The directory must be empty.

If **rmdir** fails and an **ls** of the directory does not show any file names, try **ls -la** to print files that have a dot (.) as the first character of their file name. Remove those files and then remove the directory.

Return Value

If the directory was removed, **rmdir** returns a zero exit status. Otherwise, a non-zero exit status is returned and **rmdir** displays an error message.

sleep *num*

Description

sleep suspends execution of the shell for *num* seconds. To sleep for one minute, enter

```
sleep 60
```

sleep is used within shell scripts to give the user time to read any error or warning messages.

sort [*opts*] [*file(s)*]

Description

sort sorts the lines in the file specified on the command line. If no files are specified, **sort** reads from standard input.

By default, **sort** sorts the lines in a file in ascending order. The following options can be specified to modify the sort output:

Option	Meaning
-n	Sort by numeric order.
-o *outfile*	Put the output in *outfile* instead of sending it to the standard output.
-t*c*	Use *c* as the field separator character instead of the default tabs and spaces.
+*n*	Sort on field number *n*. The **sort** command numbers fields starting with 0.
-r	Sort in reverse order.

The following examples illustrate the use of the **sort** command:

```
# Sort the employee file
$ sort employees
# Sort the employee file in reverse
  order
$ sort -r employees
# Sort the /etc/passwd file by user id
$ sort -t: +2 -n /etc/passwd
```

Return Value

A zero exit status is returned if the sort was successful. A non-zero exit status is returned and a diagnostic message is printed if **sort** fails.

tail [±*num*] [**-f**] [*file(s)*]

Description

tail prints the last part of a file. By default, the last ten lines of the specified *file* are printed. If a +*number* argument is specified, **tail** will start that many lines from the beginning of the file. If a -*number* is specified, then **tail** will begin printing at that many lines from the end of the file.

If the **-f** option is specified, **tail** will not exit when it detects an end of file, but will continue to read the file as it is growing. This option is useful for monitoring the output of commands redirected to a file with background processing.

The following examples show various uses for the **tail** command:

```
# Display the last 5 files that were
  modified
$ ls -ltr | tail -5
# Monitor the output of a background
  sort command
$ sort employees -o employee.out&
$ tail -f employee.out
```

tee [-a] *file(s)*

Description

 tee reads from standard output and writes to both the standard output and the *file(s)* specified on the command line. The -a option causes **tee** to append to the file(s).

 The following is a example of how **tee** can be used to create three files with the output of the **who** command:

```
$ who | tee who1 who2 who3
```

tr [-c][-d][-s][*string1* [*string2*]]

Description

 tr translates the characters in *string1* to those in *string2*. *string1* and *string2* may contain single characters, a group of characters enclosed in brackets, or a range of characters in the form of **a-z** also enclosed in brackets. Nonprintable characters may be specified by their octal notation (i.e., carriage return is '\012'). *string1* and *string2* should be enclosed in quotes to prevent interpretation by the shell.

 The following options can be specified to the **tr** command:

Option	*Meaning*
-c	Complements the set of characters in *string1* with respect to the character set. In other words, the -c option specifies all characters not in *string1*.
-s	Squeezes multiple occurrences of characters in *string2*.
-d	Deletes input characters specified in *string1*.

 The following example capitalizes all characters in the file *employees*:

```
$ tr "[a-z]" "[A-Z]" < employees
```

true

Description

true always returns a zero exit status. **true** is used to create an endless **while** loop:

```
while true
do
  echo "More? "
  read ans
  if [ "$ans" = "n" ]
  then
      break
  fi
done
```

Note the use of the conditional test (**if** and **break** statement to exit the loop.

Return Value

true always returns a zero exit status.

uniq [-c] [-d] [-u] [*infile* [*outfile*]]

Description

uniq eliminates any adjacent lines in a file that are duplicated. The input file should be in sorted order.

The following options can be specified to the **uniq** command:

Option	Meaning
-c	Prints a count of the number of times each line occurs in the file. The **-c** option suppresses the **-d** and **-u** options.
-d	Displays only duplicated lines.
-u	Displays only lines that are not duplicated.

uniq is useful for determining the number of times a specific line occurs in a file. For example, the following script tells how many times each word is used within a file:

```
# First, put each word on a line by
# itself
tr -cs "[a-zA-Z]" "[\012*]" < $1 >
    $1.tmpa
# Now sort the file
sort < $1.tmpa > $1.tmpb
# Then, perform a unique word count
uniq -c $1.tmpb
# And clean up the temporary files
rm -f $1.tmp?
```

wc [-w] [l] [c] [*file(s)*]

Description

wc counts the number of lines, words, and characters in a file. If a file name is not specified on the command line, **wc** reads from standard input. Otherwise, **wc** prints the counts for each file and then prints the total of lines, words, and characters for all specified files.

A **-l** causes only the number of lines to be printed, a **-w** prints only the number of words, and a **-c** prints only the number of characters.

The following shows how **wc** can be used to determine the number of files in a directory:

```
$ ls | wc -l
```

who [am i]

Description

who displays a list of users currently logged on to the UNIX system along with their terminal id and the time they logged in.

The **who am i** form prints only the information for the user logged onto the terminal from which the command was invoked. This form of the command is useful within shell scripts to determine whether the user running the script is authorized to do so:

```
set — `who am i`
case $1
in
  tom | mary | joe)
        # Authorized user
        ;;
  *)
        # Unauthorized user
        echo "Sorry"
        exit
        ;;
esac
```

INDEX